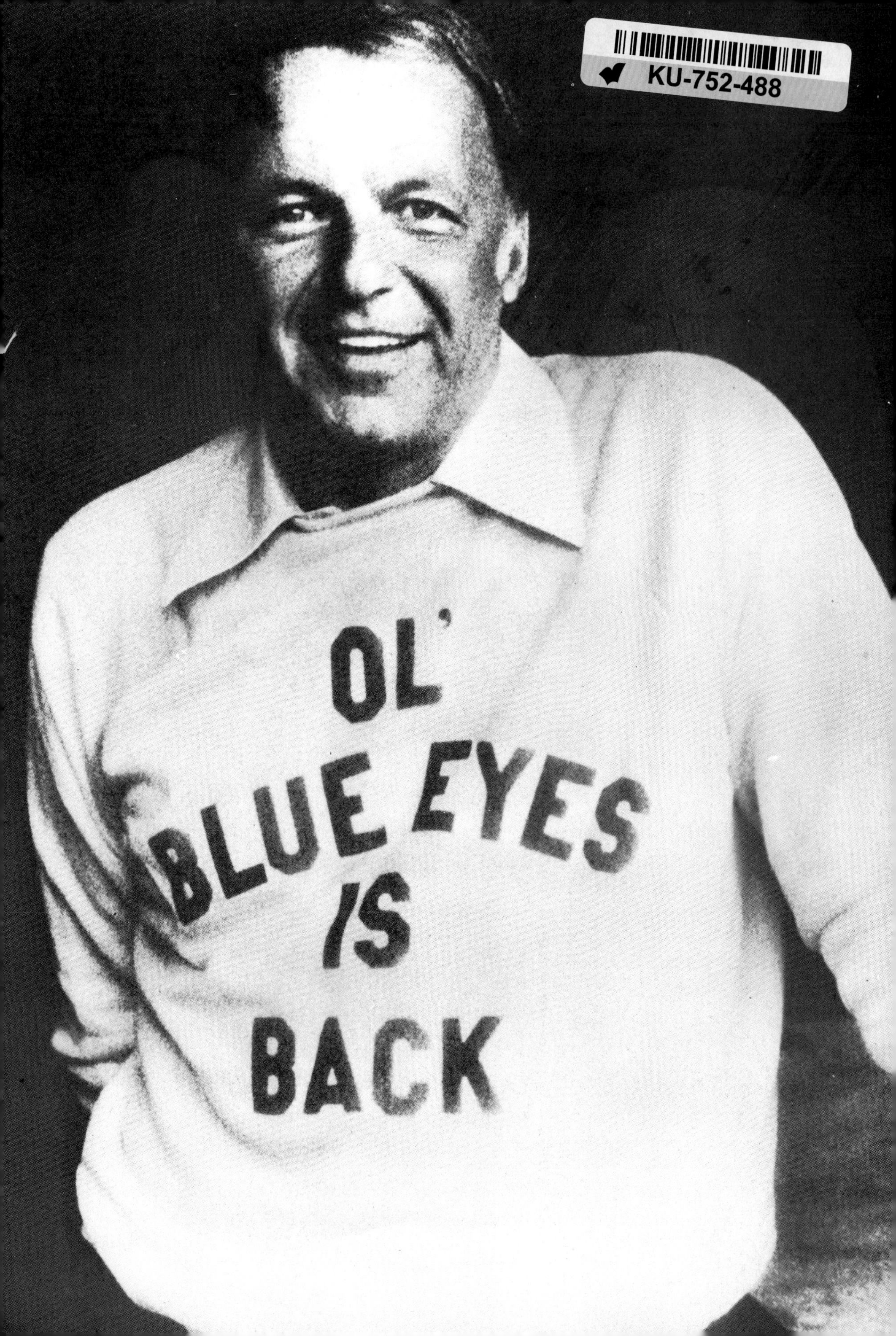
OL'
BLUE EYES
IS
BACK

Sinatra on Sinatra

Compiled by Guy Yarwood
Art directed by Mike Bell
Designed by John Gordon

W.H. Allen · London
A Howard & Wyndham Company
1982

Copyright © 1982 Omnibus Press (a division of
Book Sales Ltd, London)

Printed in Great Britain by
Wm. Clowes (Beccles) Ltd, London & Beccles
for the Publishers, W.H. Allen & Co. Ltd,
44 Hill Street, London W1X 8LB

Bound by Mackays of Chatham Ltd, Kent

ISBN 0 491 02698 6

The publishers would like to give special thanks to
Stan Britt, The Cinema Bookshop, Columbia
Pictures, Dezo Hoffman/Rex Features, London
Features International, MGM, National Film
Archive, Paramount, Pye Records, Popperfoto,
RKO, Universal Pictures, United Artists,
Warner Bros.

SINATRA ON SINATRA

— YOU'LL GET YOURS —

I'm a highly emotional person. I do things on the spur of the moment.

People often remark that I'm pretty lucky . . . Luck is only important in so far as getting the chance to sell yourself at the right moment. After that, you've got to have talent and know how to use it.

Someone said to me the other day: 'You've become the modern day gun-slinger; when you're in town there will always be someone who will have to come up to you and prove that he is faster on the draw, so to speak, than you are.' And that's the way it seems to turn out.

I can understand that people might not believe me but I really don't go looking for trouble.

Trouble just seems to come my way — unbidden, unwelcome, unneeded.

If I do anything, it'll be on the front pages of the Journal American.

Have you heard about Kim Novak's latest kick? She's selling that luxurious house of hers because she's far too comfortable there.

She says you need to have some hardships in order to be creative. Maybe I'll do that when people have had enough Sinatra one of these days. I keep telling myself it won't be much longer.

There are a handful of people who won't let go of me and won't try to be fair.

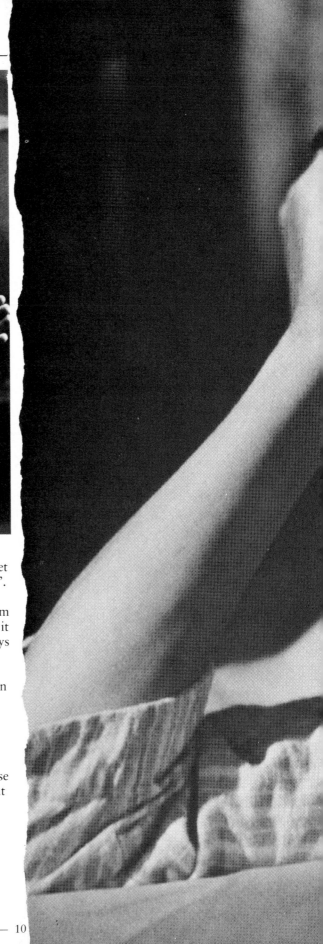

After I fly off the handle and a thing is over I feel twice as bad as when I was angry. You get to think, 'Jeez, I'm sorry that had to happen!'.

More than anything I expect and hope for from other people is kindness, and if I don't get it, it really upsets me. But then, I suppose, it always has.

I've always wanted to carry a million dollars in my pocket.

Nobody's older than me . . I'm older than water.

I wouldn't face myself poor now. Not because I'm frightened of the elements of poverty. But once you've been privileged to all this luxury . . .

I'm not a heavy thinker.

Every race produces men with big, strong muscles, and guys like me.

SINATRA ON SINATRA

— GENTLE ON MY MIND —

I'm not the kind of guy who does a lot of brainwork about why or how. I get an idea — maybe I get sore about something. And when I get sore, I do something about it . . . With grown-ups, it's not so easy — education. Kids are at a more receptive age.

. . . on his reputation for intransigence — and his reputation for not being able to take criticism . . .
Well now, let's take criticism first. People say I won't be criticised. It's not that I mind being criticised, for Chrissakes. I don't mind criticism so long as the people doing the criticism know their stuff, their facts. What infuriates me is that most of our so-called 'music critics' have got nothing in here (points to his head). No, worse still — in here (points to his ear). What I've forgotten about music they haven't learned yet.

But the real trouble comes from a few embittered columnists. I have consistently maintained that they have absolutely no right to question me on my private life if I don't want to answer their questions. Just because I am a public entertainer, I do not become the property of the press. I do get angry with the press because they will not accept this. They badger, badger, badger. And another reason I get angry is because they are so fantastically inaccurate.

One magazine did a so-called 'profile' on me which had twenty-seven major inaccuracies in it. Is that right? And I just don't think there is any excuse at all for doing what the British press do; follow me around in packed cars sprouting with telephoto lenses and things. No. I refuse to grovel to that sort of treatment. I will continue to stand up to it.

While the press behave like that, they will get nothing out of me and I want nothing out of them. You must fight back, hit them where it really hurts — like with advertising revenue. I remember one guy who wanted to interview me sent me a three page telegram. Hundreds of words, must have cost him all of thirty dollars. I couldn't understand it, but I gathered he was explaining to me why I needed the publicity. I sent him back a telegram with one word — WHAT? — and that was the last I heard from him. There — I've made my speech about the press. Now let's forget it, shall we? Of course, I admit — the trouble with me is that I get impatient. I've always been that way.

You know, I might do some great things if only I would learn not to be impatient. For instance, I admire someone who can walk away after being needled, quietly ignoring the whole thing. I really do admire them. But I can't do that myself. I'm too much of a volatile man. Yet if someone comes up and tells me I stink to my face, I respect them for it.

One night in New York there were screaming bobbysoxers all round the stage door, and a young feller came up to me and said: 'Are you Frank Sinatra?' I said yes. 'Well, you stink', he said and walked off. Anyone who takes that sort of trouble and has that sort of courage has my respect. It's the little snidey jibes that I hate. And needling. Needling's quite a different matter. It's then I start getting angry. Really angry. But then I've always been a rebel, always fought to do what I thought right or best. I shall feel very rewarded if some of what I've done musically rubs off on some youngster in the future.

Part of the whole thing is never to accept anything without question; never ignore an inner voice that tells you something could be better even when other people tell you it's OK . . .

THE BEGINNING
— FROM THIS MOMENT ON —

Forceps birth scars—no problems . . . :
People have suggested to me I ought to hide
those scars, but no. They're there, and that's
that. Why bother?

And growing pains:
I never had any brothers or sisters. In my
neighbourhood every family had twelve kids
and they fought constantly. But whenever there
was a beef or a party, you never saw such
closeness.

Two out-of-uniform police saw me walk down
the street in my new suit and accused me of
stealing it. They beat the stuffing out of me. I
was a bleeding mess and my clothes were
ruined.

There are several things I think I would have
done, if I had the chance again. I would have
been a little more patient about getting out into
the world. I would have seen to it that I had a
more formal education. I would have become
an accomplished musician, in the sense that I
would have studied formally, even if I never
used it.

. . . expelled from high school . . .
For general rowdiness.

**One Martin Sinatra, to his only son,
Francis Albert . . . :**
'Get outta the house and get a job!' I was
shocked. I didn't know where the hell to go. I
remember the moment. We were having
breakfast . . . This particular morning my
father said to me: 'Why don't you get out of the
house and go out on your own?'

What he really said was 'Get out'. And I think
the egg stuck in there about twenty minutes,
and I couldn't swallow it or get rid of it, in any
way.

My mother, of course, was nearly in tears, but
we agreed that it might be a good thing, and
then I packed up a small case that I had and
came to New York.

He was the first person in authority I had met
who didn't push other people around.
(**Mr Malloy, that is, his boss at the 'Jersey
Observer' where Francis A. first worked, as a
circulation-truck driver.**)

SINATRA WITH HIS MOTHER

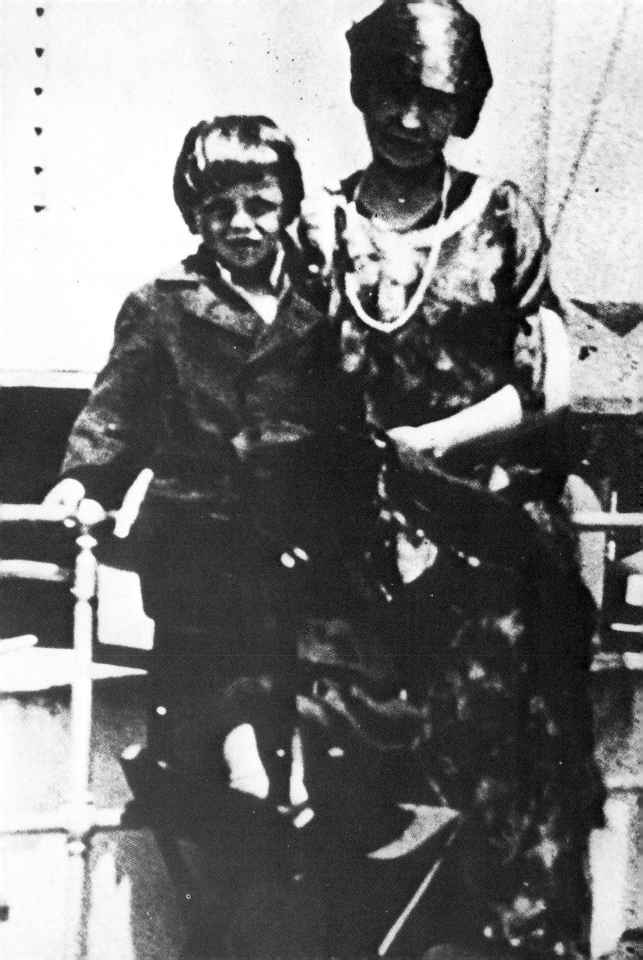

SINATRA THE SINGER

— REACHING FOR THE MOON —

Humble beginnings:
My old man thought that anyone who wanted to go into the music business must be a bum. So I packed up and left home for New York. I quit high school to do it, too.

Hard graft at the Academy of Music, 14th St.:
I'm standing there shaking, figuring that the moment they announce a guy from Hoboken, he's dead!

More hard graft and humble beginnings:
I used to sing in social clubs and things like that. We had a small group. But it was when I left home for New York that I started seriously. I was seventeen then, and I went around New York singing with little groups in road-houses. The word would get around that there was a kid in the neighbourhood who could sing. Many's the time I worked all night for nothing. Or maybe I'd sing for a sandwich or cigarettes—all night for three packets.

But I worked on one basic theory—stay active, get as much practice as you can. I got to know a song-plugger called Hank Sanicola—he's now my personal manager—and he used to give me fifty cents or a dollar some weeks to buy some food. For some reason he always had faith in me.

Radio programmes just about sustain Sinatra . . .
It sustained everybody but me. I was on four local stations and sometimes had it planned so I'd be on the air somewhere or other every three hours all through the day. But the only money I got out of the whole thing was seventy cents car fare from Jersey to the Mutual studios. On top of the eighteen sustainers a week. I landed a job at the Rustic Cabin and earned myself a three-day honeymoon with Nancy.

ALL OR NOTHING AT ALL

From Major Bowes to Harry . . .
When I started singing in the mid-1930s, putting down earlier ambitions to be either a monologist or a juggler, everybody was trying to copy the Crosby style—the casual kind of raspy sound in the throat. Bing was on top, and a bunch of us—Dick Todd, Bob Eberly, Como was coming along, Dean Martin was just starting out—were trying to break in. It occurred to me that maybe the world didn't need another Crosby.

I decided to experiment a little and come up with something different. What I finally hit on

was more the *bel canto* Italian school of singing, without making a point of it. That meant I had to stay in better shape because I had to sing more. It was more difficult than Crosby's style, much more difficult.

I won a Major Bowes Amateur Hour and after that the first job I had of any importance was with Harry James, in the summer of 1939 when he was a new, baby band and nobody had heard of him either. That was all right but in those days all the struggling singers were trying to get with either Tommy Dorsey or Glenn Miller. Miller was the hotter of the two, but the fellows I knew, almost to a man, wanted to be with Dorsey because he was a better showcase. Miller was not a 'singer's band'. Tommy was. He presented a singer in a much more specialised manner.

In his arrangements he avoided, as much as he could, having the singer stand up after the first chorus, sing the vocal, then sit down and have the orchestra finish. Tommy tried to present the singer as a specialised piece of talent with

the band. I dreamed, like all the other young boy singers around, of going with Tommy.

I didn't know it at the time — I suspected it, but I didn't know — that Tommy had his eye on me. I learned later that he was having a couple of beefs with his singer, Jack Leonard, and was scouting around for a new boy. With the James band I cut a record — I've forgotten the title — and the song plugger sent it to Dorsey.

. . . and from Harry to Tommy . . .
When I told Harry about Tommy's offer and said I wanted to leave, he just tore up my contract there and then and wished me luck. That night the bus pulled out with the rest of the boys at about half-past midnight. I'd said goodbye to them all, and it was snowing, I remember. There was nobody around and I stood alone with my suitcase in the snow and watched the tail-lights disappear. Then the tears started and I tried to run after the bus. There was such spirit and enthusiasm in that band, I hated leaving it. For maybe the first five months with Dorsey I missed the James band.

THAT SENTIMENTAL (?) GENTLEMAN

— C'EST MAGNIFIQUE! —

Tommy was very angry when I said I wanted to leave him and start out on my own. I gave him a whole year's notice, but even so he refused to speak to me for months. He just couldn't understand why anyone should want to leave him. Years after we did a one-night stand together at the Paramount Theatre, once again the best of friends.

I'll admit, it was a very big gamble for me leaving Tommy, but I guess I must have had someone watching over me from the day I was born, because I seem to have made the right move every time. You see, I figured that no one had seriously challenged Bing Crosby since 1931. There were two other guys coming up and if they had got the edge on me by even a few months, I might never have made it. When I left Tommy, I had Sanicola with me. Then I hired Axel Stordahl from Tommy to do my arranging. Tommy had paid him one hundred and fifty dollars a week—I paid him six hundred and fifty, and Tommy got even madder with me then!

What really put the clincher on my decision was when I heard that Bob Eberly was planning to break off with Jimmy Dorsey . . . Nobody had broken the ice since Crosby, and I thought that somebody is going to come along and do this any day. If Eberly got out ahead of me, I'd be in trouble.

Tommy was a very lonely man. He was a strict disciplinarian with the band—we'd get fined if we were late—yet he craved company after the shows and never really got it. The relationship between a leader and the sidemen, you see, was rather like a general and privates. We all knew he was lonely, but we couldn't ask him to eat and drink with us because it looked too much like shining teacher's apple.

Anyway, one night two of us decided to hell with it, we'd ask him out to dinner. He came along and really appreciated it. After that he became almost like a father towards me—and in spite of the fact that, being by nature a John Rebel, I was always the guy who had to pass on the beefs of the boys in the band.

One time there was a lot of unrest in the band because of travelling all night in Greyhound buses without any refreshments. So I went to Tommy and said: 'Look, the boys are unhappy—hard seats, no air, no refreshments. When they come on the stand, they're out. You won't get the best out of them like this'. After that there were always twelve cases of coke on every bus—till Joey Bushkin introduced the band to Pernod and all the coke suddenly went green.

Even without lyrics, Tommy made it sound so musical that you never lost the thread of the message.

'I REMEMBER TOMMY'

Gettin' Sentimental

I'd sit up playing cards with Tommy till maybe 5.30 every morning. He couldn't sleep ever; he had less sleep than any man I've ever known. I'd fall off to bed about then, but around 9.30a.m. a hand would shake me awake and it'd be Tommy saying, 'Hey pally—how about some golf?' So I'd totter out on to the golf course. Tommy bought a baby-carriage one day, filled it with ice and beer and hired an extra caddie to wheel it round after us. We'd have a beer after each shot. After nine holes, imagine—we were loaded.

Tommy was great at showcasting soloists and singers. Look who he had in the band then—Bunny Berigan, Ziggy Elman, Joe Bushkin, Buddy Rich—and each had their own group of fans. Tommy's presentation was superb; he'd pace and plan every band show from start to finish. I certainly learnt everything I know about phrasing and breath control from listening to the way he played that trombone.

It was a wonderful life, they were great days. I can remember every detail of them even now. But it was hard work; nine shows a day of forty-five minutes each, in which I'd sing maybe twelve songs. There were no problems, though. No warm-up even; I had real strong pipes in those days.

There was a group of Jack Leonard's fans in the band and they sort of resented a newcomer in his place. So I kept to myself. But then I've always been a loner—all my life. Eventually I shared a room with another loner, Buddy Rich, who was drummer with the band.

Funny thing is that about three years before, I'd been out dancing with Nancy at a Dorsey band-show and I was cocky, you know, and I pointed up to where Jack Leonard was sitting on the stand and said to her: 'See that singer guy? One day I'll be sitting where he's sitting'. And sure enough I was.

I'd sung in front of Dorsey once a few years before I'd joined him though. Or rather I hadn't sung! It was an audition, and I had the words on the paper there in front of me and was just going to sing when the door opened

and someone near me said 'Hey, that's Tommy Dorsey'. He was like a god, you know. We were all in awe of him in the music business. Anyway, I just cut out completely – dead. The words were there in front of me but I could only mouth air. Not a sound came out. It was terrible. When he eventually did send for me and ask me to join his band, the first thing he said was 'Yes, I remember that day you couldn't get out those words'.

From a singer's standpoint, I'd say Tommy has the band. There's a guy, now, who was a real education for me, in music, in business, every possible way. I learned about dynamics and phrasing and style from the way he played his horn, and I enjoyed my work because he always sees to it that a singer is given a perfect setting.

BOBBYSOXERS
THE THOUGHTS OF THE SULTAN OF SWOON
— I'VE GOT A CRUSH ON YOU —

Now, wouldn't it be awful for me if there weren't people around that stage-door? I can't tell you much about how I handle them. It all depends on the individual case. Some of them follow me to restaurants in taxis. I don't mind that because it doesn't go too deep.

Bobbysoxers? You don't need a head-shrinker for the explanation:
Psychologists tried to go into the reasons with all sorts of deep theories. I could have told them why. Perfectly simple: it was the war years, and there was a great loneliness. And I was the boy in every corner drug-store, the boy who'd gone off, drafted, to the war. That was all.

. . . after all, look at the kids today . . .:
I get a kick out of reading what the kids today are doing to The Beatles. They seem a little

more aggressive than they were a hundred years ago at the Paramount Theatre when the kids liked me. I'll never forget the first time I heard that strange sound in the audience – the old swooning business, I didn't know what was happening. This moaning just started, then it began to build. But I must say the kids never tried to tear me apart. In fact, they had their own police force. The girls formed a security squad to take care of me. The only time they really hurt me – and it was purely by accident – was one night when I was doing the Hit Parade on radio and doubling with a personal appearance at the Waldorf. I came out about 1 am and two girls grabbed the loose ends of my bow tie and began a tug of war. They almost tore my head off. I had a ring around my neck for weeks.

I think my appeal in those days was due to the fact that there hadn't been a troubadour around for ten or twenty years, from the time that Bing had broken in and went on to radio and movies. And he, strangely enough, had appealed primarily to older people, middle-aged people.

When I came on the scene, and people began noticing me at the Paramount Theatre, I think the kids were looking for somebody to cheer for. Also the war had just started. They were looking for somebody who represented those gone in their life.

During the show we used to let the kids ask questions – they'd ask about my parents and my wife and kids, and it was obvious that they felt I was the neighbourhood boy who made good. The press helped, too, because they printed stuff from the pro-Crosby group, who were hollering that Sinatra didn't have anything compared to their boy, and my kids would yell back, 'Yes he has, yah, yah, yah'. People began coming to hear for themselves.

I began to realise that there must be something to all this commotion. I didn't know exactly what it was, but I figured I had something that must be important.

MOBBED AT LOS ANGELES AIRPORT IN 1946

There's one girl though who's always in the audience. When I look accidentally in her direction, she lets out an awful yell. And sometimes she gets hysterical. The other morning she got that way and they told her they'd let her come up and see me. When I saw her, she was still crying. After a while she promised she'd be a good girl if I'd give her my bow-tie — you know how girls have started to wear bow-ties. So I did and she promised to be quiet. The next day, I got out on the stage and there she was yelling worse than before.

Did you know that dozens of kids have been hurt since I've been in New York this trip? And did you know that the Police Department has specifically asked me not to stop on the street any more than I can help? I'm not playing the big hero part. I just like the kids and I'll be damned before I'll see them hurt because of me.

. . . quite a turn-out, too, for that Hollywood Bowl début, in '44 . . .:
They converged on our car and practically picked it up. Musta been 5,000 kids jammed up behind the forty or fifty people mashed against the car. It was exciting. But it scares the wits out of you, too.

. . . but what about the middle-aged lady who had reportedly fainted at his gig . . .?
She was simply overcome by the heat. One of the columnists picked up the story and twisted it around.

THE BOBBYSOX BONANZA

— NEW YORK, NEW YORK —

It's always wonderful to come back to New York, well—because this always happens.

The Paramount, NYC, December 31, 1942:
That day at the Paramount, I'll never forget it. It was the day things got really started. It was my first real engagement after leaving Tommy, and the Paramount was at the time the Mecca of the entertainment world. Benny Goodman was playing there with his band and there was a Crosby picture showing, so the kids were really being pulled in. Benny had the top band in the world then and it was the first time I'd sung with him. He'd never heard anything about me, and when he introduced me he just said kind of matter of fact: 'And now—Frank Sinatra'.

Now Benny lived in a complete world of his own. All he was conscious of was his clarinet and his orchestra—nothing else. A true musician through and through. He never knew anything about new up-and-coming singers or anything like that. Anyway, when he introduced me I stuck my head and one foot out through the organdie curtains—and froze! The kids let out the loudest scream you ever heard. I couldn't move a muscle—I was as nervous as a son-of-a-bitch. Benny had never heard the kids holler before and he froze too—with his arms raised on the up-beat. He looked round over one shoulder and said, to no one in particular, 'What the ---- was that?' That somehow broke the tension and I couldn't stop laughing for the first three numbers. But for that remark of Benny's, I think I'd have been too nervous to sing at all.

A friendly warning from The Voice to his young female admirers, following mass hysteria—and all-together screaming—at the Paramount, Columbus Day, 1944 . . .:
If you've heard our shows in California, you know how nicely our girls out there behave themselves.

ARRIVING IN PASADENA

— 26 —

SINATRA THE SINGER
HONESTY IS THE BEST POLICY
— ALL OR NOTHING AT ALL —

Whatever has been said about me as a person is unimportant. When I sing, I believe . . . I'm honest.

If you want to get an audience with you, there's only one way. You have to reach out to them with total honesty and humility.

You can be the most artistically perfect performer in the world, but an audience is like a broad—if you're indifferent, endsville!

That goes for any kind of human contact, a politician on television, an actor in the movies, or a guy and a gal. That's as true in life as it is in art.

In the early 30s, we were looking for a new sound too, but not a return to the past. We went forward.

I'm flattered. I have heard many so-called imitators but I haven't heard anybody do it yet. I keep looking and listening.

DORSEY...HEIFETZ...AND THE VOICE

— DO YOU KNOW WHY? —

The thing that influenced me most was the way Tommy played his trombone. He would take a musical phrase and play it all the way through, seemingly without breathing, for eight, ten, maybe sixteen bars.

How in the hell did he do it? I use to sit behind him on the bandstand and watch, trying to see him sneak a breath. But I never saw the bellows move in his back. His jacket didn't even move. I used to edge my chair to the side a little, and peek around to watch him. Finally, after a while I discovered that he had a 'sneak' pinhole in the corner of his mouth—not an actual pinhole, but a tiny place where he was breathing. In the middle of a phrase, while the tone was still being carried through the trombone, he'd go *shhh* and take a quick breath and play another four bars with that breath. Why couldn't a singer do that too?

Fascinated, I began listening to other soloists. I bought every Jascha Heifetz record I could find and listened to him play the violin hour after hour. His constant bowing, where you never heard a break, carried the melody line straight on through, just like Dorsey's trombone.

It was my idea to make my voice work in the same way as a trombone or violin—not sounding like them, but 'playing' the voice like those instruments. The first thing I needed was extraordinary breath control which I didn't have. I began swimming every chance I got in public pools—taking laps underwater and thinking song lyrics to myself as I swam, holding my breath.

I worked out on the track at the Stevens Institute in Hoboken, running one lap, trotting the next. Pretty soon I had good breath control but that still wasn't the whole answer. I still had to learn to sneak a breath without being too obvious. It was easier for Dorsey to do it through his 'pinhole' while he played the trombone. He could control the inhalation better because the horn's mouthpiece was covering up his mouth. Try it and see, and sing at the same time.

Instead of singing only two bars or four bars of music at a time—like most of the other guys around—I was able to sing six bars without taking a visible or audible breath. This gave the melody a flowing unbroken quality and that—if anything—was what made me sound different. It wasn't the voice alone; in fact, my voice was always a little too high, I thought, and not as good in natural quality as some of the competition.

THE VOICE ON THE VOICE
— WITH EVERY BREATH I TAKE —

I had to learn to read every song the right way and make a contact with the audience. And all the time I knew the audience would say: 'How does the guy get the breath to do it?' The reason why Perry Como has had such a lasting career is that when he sings it is 2 + 2 equals 4 and the audience can see it and the audience thinks it can do the same. My success has been more specialised because no one audience can sing my way. I'd love to hear a good imitator – a good mimic – of Sinatra. But where is there

one? When I sing occasionally now it is physically ardous. Before I give a performance I have to go into training and cut down on smoking and drinking, and I play golf and I do press-ups.

I don't sing for the kids now – I never did, really. They have their special types of music, and that is good, but their music doesn't have to be mine. My son, Frank Jnr, doesn't sing their music either, although my youngest daughter, Christian, who is 16, sometimes says to me: 'Why don't you sing for the kids, Daddy?' But the other day she took a lot of my albums and played them through and said: 'You know, Daddy, you sing pretty well.' It was impromptu and she is very blunt and direct. I was very pleased . . . (1964).

ADVICE FROM THE CHAIRMAN OF THE BOARD
SINGING?
— YOU'LL KNOW WHEN IT HAPPENS —

It's like lifting weights. You're conditioning yourself.

incidentally,
If I were starting all over again, I'd get a job with a band. I would sing and sing and sing. If a leader gave me forty songs a night, I would tell him to give me sixty. There's no teacher like experience.

but . . .
You cannot swing if a band doesn't settle into the proper tempo. I don't care how good you are, it just doesn't come out right. It happens very often when you get a band that's kind of off-balance.

My favourite tempo . . .?
Any tempo, so long as the lyrics fit the cadence properly.

and how do you communicate the mood of a song, Frank . . .?
It's because I get an audience involved, personally involved in a song—because I'm involved myself . . . Being an eighteen-carat manic-depressive and having lived a life of violent emotional contradictions, I have an over-acute capacity for sadness as well as elation . . .

VOICE OF THE GUV'NOR
— MY WAY —

Over the years my voice has held up pretty good. It's deepened and darkened a bit which is fine with me because I used to think it was too high. The only time I ever lost it was in 1949 or 1950. I was doing three shows a night at the Copacabana in New York, five days a week on a Lucky Strike radio programme, live every night with Dorothy Kirsten. And I was rehearsing every day for something—benefits, concerts, etc. It was in February and I had a real bad cold, and was run down physically—my resistance was knocked out. I came out on stage at the Copa one morning about 2.30 to do the third show. I opened my mouth, and nothing came out—absolutely nothing—just dust. I was never so panic stricken in my whole life.

I remember looking at the audience—a blizzard outside, about seventy people in the place—and they knew something serious had happened. There was absolute silence—stunning, absolute silence. I looked at them, and they looked at me, and I looked at Skitch Henderson, who was playing the piano. His face was ghastly white. Finally, I turned to the audience and whispered into the microphone, 'Goodnight', and walked off the floor.

It turned out I had had a vocal-cord haemorrhage, bleeding in my throat. For days before, I had noticed speckles of blood in my mouth and I thought I had a cut gum or

I never had a vocal lesson—a real one—except to work with a coach a few times on vocal calisthenics, to help the throat grow and add a couple of notes on the top and spread the bottom. Right now, in a song, I can sing about an octave and seven, and when I vocalise I can do a little bit over two octaves.

I ran up against an F sharp the other day and I realised how much I've changed. I'd rather not sing that high note any more. I could but I don't think I should. Back in the old days when I was seventeen or eighteen, I'd wail any note in the book. I was lousy but I was fearless.

I don't know whether I have a particular favourite myself, but Nancy prefers 'This Love Of Mine'—maybe because as well as singing it, I collaborated on writing it. The only song hit I ever had.

I use all the colour changes I can get into my voice. The microphone catches the softest tone, a whisper.

My voice is as good now as it ever was. But I'll be the first to know when it starts to go—when the vibrato starts to widen and the breath starts to give out. When that happens, I'll say goodbye.

The music written today is nowhere near as good as it was ten or twenty years ago. But it's a whole new world. I have no complaint with the youngsters and their kind of music because we must stop and think that 25 years ago we made the music of our era. We liked a certain kind of music, and that's what they wrote and played for us. Kids want identity and they find their own identity. Like my daughter Tina—she's sixteen and she appreciates what I do, but she prefers the other, and I never put her down for it. Sure, there are bad songs that the kids have. They're poorly written and they have no melody, but it's another kind of music. There's certainly no harm in it.

You must pace yourself, even when you feel strong. I was never the best example of this. When we did nine shows a day at the Paramount, I went on to sing till three every morning . . . and my voice gave out for a while. I'm always worried about Sammy Davis, Jr., who never gives his throat a rest. I've warned him: 'You're going to open your mouth to sing, and dust will come out . . .'

something. Like an idiot, I hadn't even gone to the doctor. Well, he ordered me to remain absolutely silent for forty days—the toughest thing I ever did. I carried a pad and pencil around to write with. After the fortieth day, I started to talk again, very quietly, then to do a few vocal exercises. It sounded like a thirteen year old boy, like a kid in the Vienna Choir or at a barmitzvah. The voice had gone way up in the air because it had absolutely brand new vocal cords. I worked on it very gently, very carefully, and it began to settle back where it was.

Since then I've become something of a student of the throat and vocal cords. I've talked to so many doctors that I'm practically an eye, ear and throat specialist myself. I smoke too much and drink too much but I've learned that the vocal cords aren't bothered too much by that—they're in a protected part of the body. What does hurt them is over-use, abuse like shouting and not warming up properly before you sing. Every day, when I'm doing a club date or planning to record, I try to spend at least an hour at the piano, vocalising. My standard phrase is, 'Let us wander by the bay', progressing two notes at a time, up the scale and back.

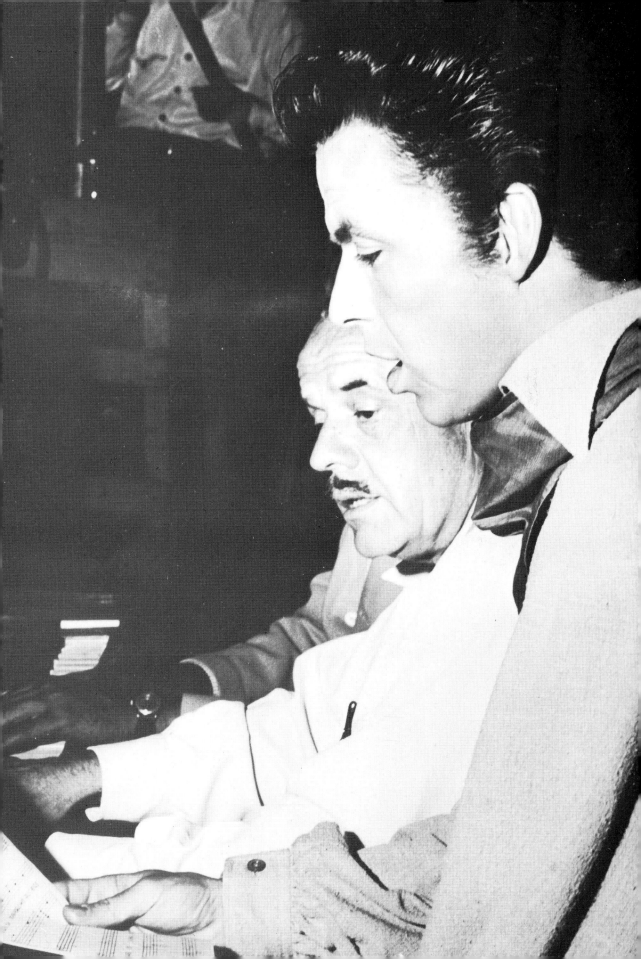

THE MICROPHONE
THE SINGER'S INSTRUMENT
— D O Y O U K N O W W H Y ? —

One thing that was tremendously important was learning the use of a microphone. Many singers never learned to use one. They never understood, and still don't, that a microphone is their instrument. It's like they were part of an orchestra, but instead of playing a saxophone they're playing a microphone.

It's difficult to explain but I think the first rule is to use it with great economy. You don't crowd it, you must never jar an audience with it, unless there's a reason to as part of a song, a comedy number or the likes. I think you must keep it as subtle as possible. A simple example is popping p's and other 'plosive sounds. They're easy to avoid. You must know when to move away from the mike and when to move

back into it. I guess a bad parallel would be that it's like a geisha girl uses her fan. To me, there's no worse sound than when a singer breathes in sharply and you hear the gasp over the microphone. The whole secret is getting the air in the corner of the mouth and using the microphone properly.

When I'm using a microphone I usually try to have a black one so that it will melt into my dinner-jacket and the audience isn't aware of it. Many years ago I found that I could take the mike off the stand and move around with it. That's a boon, and so many singers don't take advantage of it. Ella Fitzgerald, poor girl, still doesn't. They set up the mike for her and she never touches it. You can't even see her face.

TO BE PERFECTLY FRANK
— WITHOUT A SONG —

Why don't they write 'em like they used to . . .
Part of the trouble is that the great veteran song-writers, the guys who wrote the great standards, just sit back doing nothing but knocking the music of today. Rock 'n' roll belongs to the younger generation and I am not going to knock it. But you can't get Harold Arlen or Hoagy Carmichael or Harry Warren to do anything more. Sammy Cahn and Jimmy Van Heusen, and Cy Coleman and Carolyn Leigh, are the only proven song teams still producing consistently, as far as I know . . .

. . . have your fans become more sophisticated?
No, no, they didn't change. They just grew up and got older too, I guess. They got less hysterical . . . y'know?

. . . don't try to do two things at once!
You can't do justice to either. For instance, when I'm recording I'm not thinking of the movies or the night-club act.

The year: 1953:
Man, THAT was a low year.

Hey! How 'bout that spaghetti recipe you whipped up on the Dinah Shore TV Show . . .?
That was my mother's recipe. She's the one who taught me how to cook. I have a lot of her recipes.

For the next few months I'll be travelling in an ambulance but well stocked with Jack Daniels.

Never be scared of anything or anyone.

*Eh . . .??
The next four years should suffice for performing. But I'd like always to make records – that's not backbreaking! (*1962)

SINATRA ON SINATRA SONGS
— THE SONG IS YOU —

'My Way'
I loathe this song. I loathe it. A Paul Anka pop song which became a kind of national anthem.

'Mama Will Bark'
I growled and I barked on the record, but the only good it did me was with the dogs.

'The Only Couple On The Floor'
. . . Of which Sinatra said that it was nostalgic, and that it also contained:
Simpleness, sadness, sweetness.

'Send In the Clowns'
I love that song. I like it because it's an unusual song. When the hell have we had a song like that written? It's been years since Porter or one of those guys . . . even Porter I don't think put together the kind of sophistication in the lyric. Do you know people still say to me: 'I play the song fifteen-twenty times and I don't quite understand all the words'. And I just tell them one word 'A circus'. It's two people who have had a wonderful life and suddenly it's a circus. The guy runs out on the dame and she says: 'It's gonna be funny, send the clowns in because I'm gonna cry any minute'.

I've talked to singers who shall be nameless who've said to me: 'I don't understand the words'. I said: 'Because you don't read them. For Christ's sake, read the words'.

'Laura'
I once asked Cole Porter years ago — we were pretty good friends for many years — what's your favourite song? I said, 'What would you have liked to have written that you haven't written and he said 'Laura'. He said to me it's the prettiest, best melody I've heard in my life. Poor Dave Raksin never wrote anything else.

What about the lyrics to 'Strangers In The Night', Francis?
Believe it or not, I never learnt them.
(That's what he told his audience at opening of season at the Sands after his biggest-ever single smash . . .)

And a non-Sinatra song — Porter's 'Don't Fence Me In':
This song has too many words.

THIS IS MY SONG

I think there'll always be room for the singer, too. The troubadour will be around—the ballad singer—because I think the world loves a lover, and they love a guy who plays a guitar and sings pretty songs.

Even though I've been singing for a quarter of a century, and I'm the president of a major record company, I still don't have a good idea as to what the public will buy and what they won't. Music is so fragile—from day to day—that you never know.

I get about five hundred new songs a year sent to me, and chances are four hundred and ninety seven will be lousy. But I look at them all, anyway. There's always the chance one good one will come in over the transom. I got 'Young At Heart' and 'Witchcraft' that way. Five or six singers had already turned down 'Young At Heart' when I heard it.

Of course, it works the other way, too. A guy came to me with a song he was sure would be a big hit. I looked it over and threw it back. I told him it was pretentious and a piece of nothing. Nat Cole made a little recording of it, 'Mona Lisa'.

And one day Bill Holden came up to me in the studio and said he had just finished a picture which had a beautiful theme that I ought to record. I listened and I told him it was over-arranged and worthless. That was 'Love's A Many-Splendoured Thing'. Any questions?

I've heard some marvellous melodies in my lifetime as a singer, good tunes, but the words were lousy.

I work with lyrics primarily and I use the melody as a curtain, as a background. Yet I integrate it as much as I can because I want the

audience to hear what I'm saying wordwise and because I believe in the written word first — always that.

I don't read a note of music. I learn songs by having them played for me a couple of times while I read the lyrics. I can pick up the melody very quickly. I learn the lyrics by writing them out in longhand.

When I get a new song, I look for continuity of melody that in itself will tell a musical story. It must go somewhere. I don't like it to ramble. And then, by the same token, I like almost the same thing — more, as a matter of fact, in the lyrics. They must tell you a complete story, from 'once upon a time' to 'the end'.

To give an example, I believe the new song 'People' from 'Funny Girl', has never been a legitimate big hit because after the first 16 measures I think it rambles. The song gets lost somewhere. And then 'Julie' (composer Jules Styne) comes back to the original theme. The front end of it and the coda are damn good, but you get lost in between. I don't know whether he overwrote, or whether he didn't quite know how to get out of it, but it's a case in point.

When a song doesn't follow in continuity, it doesn't continue to hold the interest of an artist. And the only time that songs hold the interest of the public is when an artist, like Streisand, understands the song and sings it properly. Throughout my career, if I have done anything, I have paid attention to every note and every word I sing — if I respect the song. If I cannot project this to a listener, I fail. That's why I try to hand-pick material, so that I think an audience will immediately become attuned when they hear it. We miss many times, we all do.

THE NOW GENERATION
(VINTAGE 1968)
— YOUNGER THAN SPRINGTIME —

The young people in pop music who cannot read/write music:
I deplore their dropping out of school. It's a shame they're not fully educated. Their creative output now is so enormous and suddenly they're at the top of the charts, they're deluged with activity, but they are not prepared.

Is Sinatra part of the Now Generation?
When all this began, I felt left out. I wondered what was going to happen to people like me. I couldn't compromise with the New Sound. I just sat on the side-lines waiting it out.

I began to feel that there must be a way for me to be a part of it. Five years ago I said that in five years' time something would congeal from the early skull-rattling sound. It congealed. Today the young songwriters are more ballady than even Rodgers and Hart. I don't feel like such an outsider.

The lyrics of the kids these days are poignant and sweet. It almost goes back to early-American days. Their thing is a form of poetry, or lyricism. Lyricism is what I've done all my life.

The kids are unhip as compared to a few years ago when they were going through the protest thing. Now there's a kind of sadness to their lyrics, yet they're so young. They're like people

of around forty or fifty. They are sad and quite serious. Their genre is really the cowboy lament.

There's an undertone going back to the old blues structure—in their lyrics more than in their music. It fits their own demeanour. It's not a hokey-pokey sort of sadness. They are saddened by the world, by poverty, by the war. And their message has gotten through to their parents.

Where does the Now Sound take us . . .?
Their songs are already standards. It will settle in ten to fifteen years to a new style. I wouldn't be surprised if it evolves into serious music that will be played in the repertoires of symphony orchestras.

POP SONGS-
GREAT 'N' LOUSY
— WHO TOLD YOU I CARE? —

A Sinatra resolution, mid-1950's:
. . . not to sing any songs that do not possess musical and lyrical merit. In the past—though not the recent past—I would often be persuaded to record or broadcast an inartistic number on the grounds that it was 'commercial'. I can see now that I should not have given in to this kind of pressure, because it was harmful to the kind of reputation I want to maintain, and also to show-business in general. If singers and bands would refuse to touch most of to-day's miserable output of popular music, even at the risk of losing a fast buck, the songwriters and publishers would just have to put on their thinking caps and provide something better! Meanwhile, I'm happy to be stuck with a repertoire almost exclusively made up of standard songs. These will still sound good when every current gimmick is forgotten. Even in the symphonic field there aren't so many works dating from the Twenties as well as 'Blue Room', 'My Heart Stood Still', 'You Do Something To Me', 'Ol' Man River' and others of that standard . . .

About the popular songs of the day, they've become so decadent, they're bloodless . . . Outside of production material, show tunes,

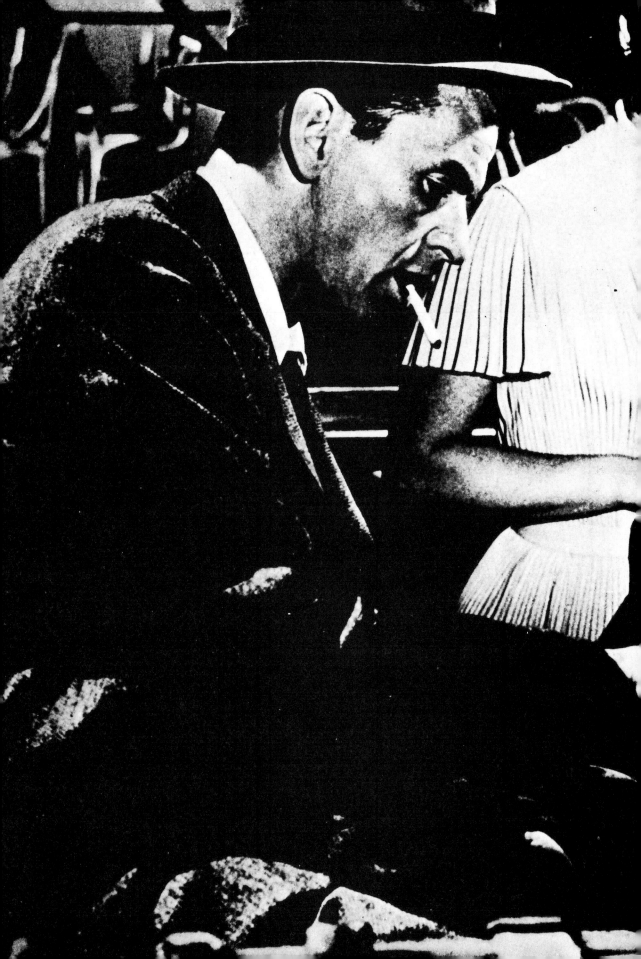

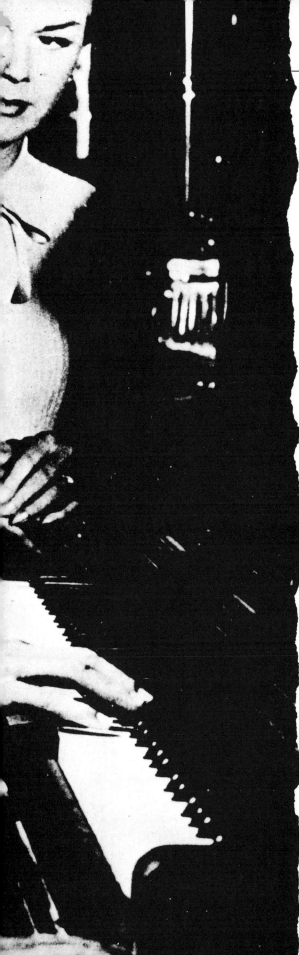

you can't find a thing. All you get is a couple of songs like 'Apple Blossom Wedding' and 'Near You' . . . (censored).

If the music business is to lead the public—and actually we do lead it as to the thing it likes—we must give people things that move them emotionally, make them laugh, too. But we're not doing it and there's something wrong someplace.

I don't think the music business has progressed enough. There are a lot of people to blame for this. The songwriter in most cases finds he has to prostitute his talents if he wants to make a buck. That's because not enough publishers are buying the better kind of music. The publisher is usually a fly-by-night guy anyway and so to make a few fast bucks he buys a very bad song, very badly written. And the recording companies are helping those guys by recording such songs . . . If they turned them down, it wouldn't do them any harm and it might do music some good . . .

You know, I talk to a lot of kids. They're pretty smart; they've been around buying records and listening to bands. They don't like those bad songs, at least not the kids with whom I speak individually.

I'd like to see popular music brought into grammar and high schools as part of the education, if the proper people were teaching it . . . With all the people in the music business, we could get enough people to go to so many schools each year and explain the inner intricacies of making a hit song . . . and a good song . . . and a poor song.

(c. late 1940's)

SONGS FOR SWINGIN' SINATRA

— I'VE HEARD THAT SONG BEFORE —

The melody should be like a backdrop for the lyrics. Sure, it should be good and musical. But it should be more like a guy reading poetry with organ music or something going in the back. If the poem or lyrics are stated often enough with the same music going on at the same time, they become associated as one.

Of course the lyrics have to be something special, like the ones that Larry Hart and Oscar Hammerstein and Ira Gershwin and Johnny Mercer and Sammy Cahn have been writing. You know, I have a healthy respect for anybody who can write. I don't mean just songs. I mean anything. Sure wish I could!

One thing they're certainly not writing these days is many good lyrics. I know that because I'm more conscious of the words in songs than I am of the melody.

If what I did at Bill Miller's did anything, it convinced me once and for all that you can still show good taste and be appreciated. You don't have to sing loud and raucously and belt them over the head all the time. You can use a little restraint and try to create a mood that you and they can both feel, sort of like being together in a small room, and if you really mean it, and show that you mean it, you can register all right.

It made me feel great the way they paid attention to the songs I sang. They were good songs—all of them—at least I think so, because they were my favourites. Things like Rodgers and Hart and Rodgers and Hammerstein and the Gershwins and Cole Porter. They don't write many songs like that today . . .

Is it fair to compare today's (younger) songwriters with the great standard composers of the past . . .?
I think it's unfair now because they're too young. They haven't had a background yet. Those other guys wrote until they were seventy years old. Berlin, for Christ's sake, was writing when he was seventy-five years old. But I don't see why these kids shouldn't be as big or bigger. And something else I'd like to see happen . . .

and I see it in small areas. For instance, that great piece that that youngster wrote with a symphony orchestra. I see this kind of contemporary sound being used in symphonic arrangements and I adore it. It's a groovy idea that they do that. They're adding more guitars and more instruments that they've never used before. It's wild; it's a wonderful sound. I'd like to see more young guys take a shot at it.

What the hell can they lose? Go away for three months and get buried somewhere and write something that runs like two or three movements. It would be groovy.

ASPECTS OF RECORDING

If I make a bad record it hurts me far more than it hurts the public.

The main problem with records is finding the right material. Once a number's been chosen it doesn't really take more than forty-five minutes studio time to record. But on an off day I've been known to go on for hours at a song.

A Frank admission . . .

Some of my recent work for Capitol has lacked some of the spark it might have had. It's a long story that I don't particularly want to go into. But you're a writer and I'll bet you can't give your best when you're not happy with the people you're writing for. I wasn't happy during that period with Capitol and I'm afraid some of those later albums show it – definitely

they do. I had said I wanted to quit Capitol even if it meant not recording at all for two years until the contract ran out. But they let me go on condition I cut four more albums for them to wind up the deal. I wanted to form my own record company and run it along my own ideas.
(1961)

Set 'em up, Joe . . .

I'm working on another thought – a complete saloon album. I want to call the album 'She Shot Me Down'. It's the line from 'Bang Bang' that Sonny Bono wrote. Nancy recorded it years ago. Every one of the songs will be an out-and-out saloon song. They will be tear jerkers and cry-in-your-beer kind of things.

I've been recording my brains out. Right now, I wouldn't care if I never saw another disc.

RECORDING

— TOO MARVELLOUS FOR WORDS —

You know, I adore making records. I'd rather do that than almost anything else. You can never do anything in life quite on your own, you don't live on your own little island. I suppose you might be able to write a poem or paint a picture entirely on your own, but I doubt it. I don't think you can ever sing a song that way, anyway. Yet, in a sort of a paradoxical way, making a record is as near as you can get to it – although, of course, the arranger and the orchestra play an enormous part. But once you're on the record singing, it's you and you alone. If it's bad and gets criticised, it's you who's to blame – no one else. If it's good, it's also you. With a film it's never like that; there are producers and script-writers and hundreds of men in offices and the thing is taken right out of your hands. With a record, you're IT. But I must admit something – I'd never argue with someone like Nelson on a record date. It's his date, he's the leader.

First I decide on the mood for the album, perhaps pick a title. Or sometimes it might be that I had the title and then picked the mood to fit it. But it's most important there should be a strong creative idea for the whole package, so to speak. Like 'Only The Lonely' or 'No One Cares' for instance. Then I get a short list of maybe sixty possible songs, and out of these I pick twelve and record them.

Next comes the pacing of the album, which is vitally important; I put the titles of the songs on twelve bits of paper and juggle them around like a jigsaw until the album is telling a complete story lyric-wise. For example, the album is in the mood of 'No One Cares' – track one. Why does no one care? Because there's 'A Cottage for Sale' – track two. (That song's the saddest song ever written, by the way – it depicts the complete break-up of a home). So on right through to the last track, which might be 'One For My Baby And One More For The Road' – the end of the episode. We did in fact end the 'Only The Lonely' album with that song, and something happened then which I've never seen before or since at a record session. I'd always sung that song before in clubs with just my pianist Bill Miller backing me, a single

spotlight on my face and cigarette, and the rest of the room in complete darkness. At this session the word had somehow got around that there were about sixty or seventy people there, Capitol employees and their friends, people off the street, anyone. We had kept this song to the last track of the session. Dave Cavanaugh was the A&R man and he knew how I sang it in clubs, and he switched out all the lights bar the spot on me. The atmosphere in that studio was exactly like a club. Dave said 'Roll 'em', there was one take, and that was that. The only time I've known it happen like that.

Anyway, to get back to pacing the album – Tommy Dorsey did this with every band-show he played. Paced it, planned every second from start to finish. He never told me this; it just suddenly came to me as I sat up on that stand night after night. But this is what I've tried to do with every album I've ever made.

SINATRA SNIPPETS
FROM INSIDE THE RECORDING STUDIO
— TALK TO ME, BABY —

That record may get everyone here arrested.

We'll dedicate the next song to Ben-Gurion and call it 'There Will Never Be Another Jew'

Anyone who says I can't sing this song's got a busted reed.

I think I broke my gadarum.

I got a broken mirror in my throat. Let's have a jigger of brandy; it's cold up here. And some coffee to make it legitimate.

Man, I really got my Charlie Barnet reed on tonight!

My old man warned me about nights like these. But then he was a drinking man and he wouldn't know the difference.

Don't just sit there watching me.
Do something.

SINATRA-isms

— SOMEWHERE ALONG THE WAY —

What do I believe in—my own religious feelings? First; I believe in you and me. I'm like Albert Schweitzer and Bertrand Russell and Albert Einstein in that I have a respect for life—in any form,

I believe in nature, in the birds, the sea, the sky, in everything I can see or that there is real evidence for. If these things are what you mean by God, then I believe in God.

But I don't believe in a personal God to whom I look for comfort or for a natural on the next roll of the dice.

I'm not unmindful of man's seeming need for faith. I'm for anything that gets you through the night, be it prayer, tranquillisers, or a bottle of whisky.

Several years ago I couldn't have bought my way into a film—and today I own my own company.

Time takes care of things, but I've had bad times. Once I was on the skids. I was my own worst enemy.

My singing went downhill and I went downhill with it, or vice versa. Nobody hit me in the throat, or choked me with a necktie. It happened because I paid no attention to how I was singing. I wanted to sit back and enjoy my success and sign autographs and bank the heavy cash.

But nobody who is successful can afford to sit back and enjoy it. That I found out the hard way. Enjoyment is just a by-product of success. That's what I had to learn.

Get off your clyde and get ourselves some clydes.

It's A Wonderful World . . . well, sometimes . . .
The career is going ahead wonderfully. People are wonderful to me and I'm a happy, happy man.

Man, they have been wonderful years. Everything has really jived for me.

In your teens, there's always someone to spit on your dreams.

Man, I feel eight feet tall. Everything is ahead of me, I'm on top of the world. I'm buoyant.

SINATRA: THE MAIN INFLUENCES
(1) CROSBY
— YOU TURNED MY WORLD AROUND —

Somebody said that the Groaner could be President of the United States if he so desired. I'd like to make one correction on that statement: that guy would be President of the WORLD!
(1948)

Bing was my first singing idol—and still is. He'll always be tops. For that matter, there's no comparison between us. We're entirely different in style.

(2) BILLIE HOLIDAY
— LADY DAY —

With a few exceptions, every major pop singer in the US during her generation has been touched in some way by her genius. It is Billie Holiday whom I first heard in 52nd Street clubs in the early 30's, who was and still remains the greatest single musical influence on me.

Thanks for the songs, Paul Anka . . .
You've got so much goddamn talent you're a pain in the ass. Signed 'The Old Man'.

Thanks for the Memory, Mr Hope . . .
I couldn't get a job until Bob came along with his first TV spec. In 1950 there weren't many people around like him. People were frightened of me . . . But Hope! He and his writers wrote his entire spec. around me. I didn't get a lot of money but the show was of tremendous psychological help to me.

FRANK SINATRA AND BING CROSBY

FRANK SINATRA, BOB HOPE, BING CROSBY, JOAN COLLINS AND DEAN MARTIN

TONY, LENA, JUDY, ELLA
AND TELLING A STORY
— YOU NEVER HAD IT SO GOOD —

For my money, Tony Bennett is the best singer in the business, the best exponent of a song. He excites me when I watch him—he moves me. He's the singer who gets across what the composer has in mind, and probably a little more. There's feeling in back of it. Vic Damone has better pipes than anybody, but he lacks the know-how or whatever you want to call it. Take Lena Horne, for example, a beautiful lady but really a mechanical singer. She gimmicks up a song, makes it too pat.

TONY BENNETT

Two singers who have excited all of us, and still do as a matter of fact—Judy Garland and Ella Fitzgerald—are technically two of the worst singers in the business. Every time I see Judy I fall down, and of course Ella is my all-time favourite, but they still sing wrong. I've heard Ella sing one word, then take a breath, then sing a word with two syllables. This violates all the rules of singing. Judy does the same thing.

They forget they're telling the story in a song lyric. It doesn't flow. Now, sometimes it doesn't have to, such as in a rhythm song. You

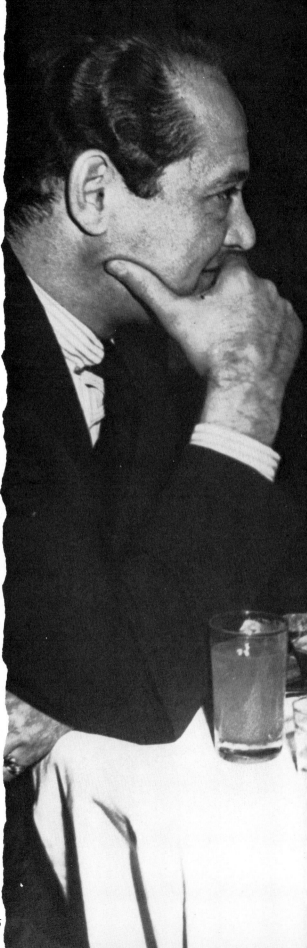

don't have to pay much attention to the lyric. But it's of vital importance when you sing something like 'Fools Rush In', or any of the great ballads. You're telling a story.

Let's say you sing four measures, and the next two measures will lyrically enhance the first four, then you sing six measures. And then, in the next instance, you may only want to, or only have to, sing one bar because there are two or three words in that measure that are completely unrelated to the other phrases. But by the same token, in your next breath you may want to sing eight full measures, because they may tell the whole point of the story.

It's just like reading poetry. And that's odd because poetry bores me. It always has. I'm one of the worst readers in the world. But when I do it in a song, I find that I enjoy it, and I find that I understand the distance necessary per phrase.

It has always surprised me that people who are so good, like Ella and Judy, do not dig this and forget the poetry. Ella, this wonderful lady, is not too commerical either. She indulges herself recording things like the old Cole Porter one called 'Down In The Depths On The 90th Floor'. I'll sing the '90th Floor' for you at your house at a party and knock you out but I wouldn't put it in a record album.

SOME OF SINATRA'S SPECIAL SINGERS
— YOU DO SOMETHING TO ME —

Another woman who isn't too commercial, either, but who nevertheless is marvellous, is Sarah Vaughan. Sassy irritated me for a long while because she was experimenting for the past ten years or so, at the expense of those of us who listened to her. She was groping around, searching for a style, for a musical identity. She finally found it, and it was deceptively simple—just straight singing with very little of that wandering around in the upper stratosphere that she used to do. It's the hardest thing for any of us to discover the art of straight, pure singing. It's easier to find a gimmick and hang on to it. I listen.

SARAH VAUGHAN

Sammy Davis Jr., is one of the most gifted entertainers and one of the most successful. I've known him since he was a child performer travelling the vaudeville and club circuit with his uncle and father and living out of trunks.

My affection for him reaches beyond his great talent and touches human qualities that would move me regardless of who possessed them.

To me, he represents the finest traditions in our business. His talents are so staggering that each time I see him I experience a greater thrill. I have said I wouldn't follow this man to any club or theatre, anywhere, not for all the gold in Las Vegas. I am proud of his fabulous success, which he has earned the hard way and fully deserves . . .

Sassy is so good now that when I listen to her I want to cut my wrists with a dull razor. Peggy Lee's pretty good with the lyrics. She sustains a little more than the other girls do. One of the greatest women singers for technique is Jo Stafford. She can hold notes for sixteen bars if she has to. She's fantastic—perfect pitch, absolutely perfect pitch. Rosie Clooney sings well. But most women have a tendency to get too breathy when you listen to their records. Maggie Whiting used to sound like she had asthma. (1965)

Of the male newcomers, Jack Jones is the best potential singer in the business. He has a distinction, an all-round quality that puts him *potentially* about three lengths in front of the other guys. He sings jazz pretty good, too. But he's got to be handled very carefully from here on out. The next year is going to tell. One thing, he should stop singing those gasoline commercials that they play on the Dodger baseball broadcasts . . . (1965)

SOLVING THE RIDDLE

It was a happy marriage. Nelson had a fresh approach to orchestration and I made myself get into what he was doing.

Nelson is the greatest arranger in the world. A very clever musician, and I have the greatest respect for him. He's like a tranquilliser—calm, slightly aloof. Nothing ever ruffles him. There's a great depth somehow to the music he creates. And he's got a sort of stenographer's brain. If I say to him at a planning meeting, 'Make the eight bar sound like Brahms', he'll make a cryptic little note on the side of some scrappy music sheet and, sure enough, when we come to the session the eighth bar will be Brahms. If I say, 'Make like Puccini', Nelson will make exactly the same little note and that eight bar will be Puccini all right and the roof will lift off. Nelson's quality of aloofness and way of detachment gives him a particular kind of disciplinary air at sessions and the band respect him for it.

Well, musically speaking, do you know what I really am? A frustrated conductor. I've been saying to Nelson for two years: 'Give up all this popular stuff. Give it up for six months and I'll commission you to write a complete concerto for the Spanish guitar so I can conduct it. Feature it in new settings, give it new sounds'. Nelson is always very interested—he'd do it better than anyone. But so far we've both been too busy to do anything more about it.

Recording with the Fat Man . . .
Recording with Billy May is like having a cold shower or a bucket of cold water thrown in your face. Nelson will come to the session with all the arrangements carefully and neatly worked out beforehand. But with Billy you sometimes don't get the copies of the next number until you've finished the one before—he'll have been scribbling away in some office in the studio right up till the start of the session.

Billy works best under pressure. So does Nelson, in fact, but not quite such hot pressure. I myself can't work well except under pressure. If there's too much time available, I don't like it—not enough stimulus. And I'll never record before eight in the evening. The voice is more relaxed then.

Billy handles the band quite differently from Nelson or Gordon. With Nelson, for instance, if someone plays a wrong note, he'll hold up his hand and stop them and say quietly, 'Now in bar sixteen you'll see it says the brass come in half a note after the woodwinds', or something like that. But Billy—there he'll be in his old pants and sweat-shirt, and he'll stop them and he'll say, 'Hey, cats—this bar sixteen. You gotta go ommpa-de-da-da-che-Ow. OK? Let's go then, cats'. And the band will go. Billy is driving, Nelson has depth, with Gordon Jenkins it's all so beautifully simple that to me it's like being back in the womb. That 'No One Cares' album I did with Gordon is the hell of an album.

. . . and with Robert Farnon:
My, he's certainly some writer.

Meet the arrangers:
A lot of singers I know never even meet their arranger. They don't know who the hell he is. That's wrong. I've worked with almost everybody in the business. I've learned so much with these guys. They're all great—Gordon, Quincy Jones, Nelson Riddle, Billy May and Johnny Mandel. They give me a boost when you sit and you think that they put all these notes down on paper for every instrument and they do it in sometimes forty-five minutes.

MY FAVOURITE BANDS?
— R I N G - A - D I N G D I N G —

F.A. Sinatra . . . and all that jazz:
I think in the next five or ten years the trend will change again, to what I don't know but I think it will change again. I think it'll go back to something more melodic then we have now. Actual jazz, real good jazz, the jazz that we think is fine jazz, good music, is dead.

The era of cool jazz is gone. I think it's absolutely dead and buried. If any kind of jazz continues, and I pray it always will, I think it will continue in the sense of what we called in the early-30s 'swing'. I think there may come to pass a period of music that will be a combination of the big-band sounds with the small-group sounds in a simple metric fashion. In other words, the skull-rattling piano sound, where the kids play up on the treble keys,

where they play triplets all the time, I think that will disappear. I think they'll go back to more of the 4/4 tempo, like the Benny Goodman swing, the basic stuff.

Hey, Mister Goodman . . .!
There's one story I must tell you about Benny. As I said, he lives only for his clarinet. One night I remember the boys in the band took a hotel room and gave a dinner for him—you know, invited along a small group to play for dancing and so on. This was long before Benny was married, so they invited a good-lookin' broad along for him. The boys had never seen him dance before; he'd always been too busy with his clarinet. But eventually he thought he'd better ask this broad to dance, so the two of them got on the floor and, after a few steps, all the boys broke up laughing—Benny's right hand was unconsciously playing the clarinet fingering of the tune up and down this broad's spine . . .

MY FAVOURITE BANDS?
— YES INDEED! —

. . . well, here's a couple . . .
The Duke, of course. I played three days at a theatre in Hartford when Ellington was there, and believe me, it was one of the biggest kicks of my life. But from a singer's standpoint I'd say Tommy was the band. The man was a real education for me, in music, in business, in every way possible. From the way he played his horn I learned about dynamics, style and phrasing; and because he always sees to it that his singers are given a perfect setting, working with him was a delight.

. . . and, of course, don't forget the Count . . .!
This is the greatest orchestra at any time in the history of the world.

. . . And I Remembered Tommy With
'I Remember Tommy'
I really think it has some of the best work I've ever done. I feel sentimental over Dorsey even after twenty years. I tried to sing the songs as he used to play them on his trombone. But we didn't put a trombone solo on the record because nobody has ever been able to recreate Tommy's particular sound. Instead we feature a trombone quartet. Sy Oliver's orchestrations are brilliant, full-blooded things. They're all Tommy's special songs, too; I haven't sung songs like these for years. They were a real lesson in elocution and diction; if I breathed in some of those long lyric lines I'd have wrecked the whole thing. The extraordinary thing is I have never heard anyone else sing Tommy's theme song 'I'm Getting Sentimental over You', maybe because it's such a hell of a difficult song to sing. One day I think I'm going to do another album called 'I Still Remember Tommy'!

AROUND THE WORLD
CHARITABLY

LONDON BY NIGHT: A memorable Sinatra charity concert, at the Royal Festival Hall, June 1962—nine years after his previous London appearance, and near to the end of an eminently successful world tour to benefit underprivileged children . . .
In a way, the whole tour has been leading up to this night. This is the climax to the whole tour. I want London to remember this night. I'm going to give them the full treatment, throw everything at them.

What a night for me that was. It's a marvellous place to sing in. Acoustically it must be perfect. You can hear your voice coming back at you and when it sounds good it helps you on further. If I never sing another note, I'll always remember that night as something special.

SOUTH OF THE BORDER: The event which precipitated the 1962 world charity tour, of which the above was a part . . .
Last year I took Nelson and forty musicians to Mexico. What a wild time we had! This was nothing to do with the government—this was out of my own pocket, to help some rehabilitated children down there. Hospitals, things like that. We planned to do one show, ended up by doing five. This was really an experience for us all. They gave me a medal, and a boy came up on the stage to pin it on me. He had no hands, only metal claws, and he took it out of the box, unclasped it and pinned it on to my coat. Five thousand people were sitting in that place and you could have heard a pin drop. I can tell you—there was a big lump in my throat . . . Then when we left there were maybe five hundred people at the airport, at nine in the morning. They all sang 'La Golondrina'—that's their farewell song—with guitars. The President of Mexico invited me to lunch and told me he wished the United States would send twenty-one performers round all the other States of Latin-America; it would do so much good. And he's right, you know. I'm sure trips like that do a tremendous lot of goodwill between countries and for international relations generally. I'd like to do more of them. But I'm getting older, and less ambitious. And a bit lazy, too, I suppose . . .

IT'S SO NICE TO GO TRAV'LING. . .
. . . and the germ of that idea might have emanated from a 1955 conversation he had with a reporter—on location, and on his 40th birthday—during which Sinatra said he'd like to visit each of the world's capital cities—including Moscow—to put on shows for the benefit of children in each of the countries. The idea was for him to travel with two major US American entertainers
. . . a name they all recognise, like Gary Cooper or Marilyn Monroe. The tour could be set up through variety clubs, which have branches in foreign countries. I understand Nehru is a member. If it could be arranged. I'd like to do it in Moscow, too.

TO LOVE AND BE LOVED . . .Touring the world in aid of childrens' charities, 1962:
I found out a lot of things I didn't know before. It was a revelation. I hope to do the same thing every year or eighteen months. It's a most gratifying experience.

Just incorporate my basic philosophy. I'm taking the trip because it gives me great personal satisfaction. I enjoy it.

Someone has tried to figure how much we made on this tour. It was something like a million dollars. I wish it was five million.

This work gives one a nice feeling. I have felt deeply about children all my life but this is the first time I have been able to get out and do anything about it.

We hope we can make these tours every year and a half or so. Maybe Scandianavia next time.

. . . including a particularly touching visit to the Sunshine Home For Children in Middlesex.
This is a lesson to grown-ups who gripe. Children like this always seem so cheerful and happy.

. . . where, amongst others, he met Johnny, a blind kid, who asked Sinatra whether he might stand on his hands for him . . .
No Johnny, I don't think you should do that for me. You might get hurt.

. . . and sensing the child's obvious disappointment, he suggest something else:
But I tell you what—let's you and me be buddies, huh?

... and, in conclusion ...
I have always had this same deep feeling about children. But it's the first time I have had the chance to get out and do something.

I want it to be a pattern of my life.

I've had a marvellous time.

But one black spot: following Sinatra's Israel concerts, his records and pictures were banned in Lebanon and Iraq ...
If this is true, I am deeply disappointed that statesmen anywhere would condemn anyone for aiding children of whatever faith or origin.

In Israel, my recent tour there was to raise money for an inter-faith youth centre in Nazareth, a primarily Arab centre, where the recipients will be primarily Arab children. My world tour, which included Israel, was dedicated to benefiting children of all faiths. I had hoped that adults everywhere had one thing in common—a love for all children.
(1962)

SINATRA IN LONDON

... and questions are asked about his movements in and around the British capital—outside of his professional reasons for being there, to make a film—to the extent that he makes himself something of a furtive recluse ...

Why, for instance, did you have to leave your London flat by the tradesmen's entrance?
First, I think it is my privilege and my business to decide exactly how I want to leave the building in which I live. If I want to leave by helicopter from the roof it is my business and no one else's.

But the reason for leaving by the tradesmen's entrance was this—on the first morning there were thirty or forty photographers crowding round the front door. Now it may seem funny and unlikely, but I just can't stand photographers in an undisciplined mass. They make me nervous and uneasy.

I can understand exactly how Prince Philip feels. There comes a limit.

Also, why do you always refuse to give a press conference in London?
In my films, on my records, in my concerts, I have always given all of myself to the public. All of myself – all I have. Every fibre. If they like what I give, OK. If they don't, I've failed.

But I think any star, like any other human being, is entitled to make his own decisions about his private life when he is not, so to speak, on show. I guard my privacy jealously. Because if I didn't, I would have no privacy left.

I am not some bosomy starlet. I don't need to fall in with the demands of the ritual publicity machine. I want to be judged on what I do artistically.

If the public don't like what I give them professionally, then I accept their judgement. But I don't have to give interviews or pose for pictures to get the public to like me. The public are more intelligent than that.

What can I say in an interview that could possibly increase my stature as a singer and actor? As I say, leave it to the public to judge. They know, they are not deceived by phoney publicity pictures. Or by show-business people airing their views on everything from Vietnam to birth control.

. . . and why all the rigmarole of arriving at Prestwick, then going to Northolt by private plane?
I personally did not choose that method of arrival. It was chosen by Brad Dexter who is producing the film which we are making here in London. I simply said to him that it would be better if I didn't arrive at London Airport as a normal passenger as I remember the scenes of confusion that have happened there when I have arrived in the past.

I hate crowds jostling me. I even get claustrophobic in elevators. Brad knows this. So he fixed for me to arrive at Northolt. And whatever they say in Parliament they knew it was me who was coming in and they gave permission. In fact, the first time I knew it was

Northolt was when some guy in RAF uniform came up, saluted and said, 'Good evening, sir'.

Look I didn't ask for smoked-glass windows in any car. The film company uses seven cars, and Brad Dexter thought that as a lot of cars in London have smoked-glass windows to give the occupants privacy, the one we used should have smoked-glass windows too.

The point is this – we just don't happen to like being stared at. And there's no doubt that smoked-glass windows do give you a lot more privacy, even though I've never had them in any of my cars before.

Anyway, is it such an awful crime to want privacy in your car?

I choose London to make this picture in because I felt it was a city that would respect that decision. I love London. I love the people here. That is why I've rented this flat in Grosvenor Square for fifty years. Because I want to come back again and again. I want the kids to use it. I want Mia to use it. But I want to be treated like a normal person . . . please, please, please, just let me be treated like a normal person.

BROADS

— MY KIND OF GIRL —

I believe in giving a woman a lot of time to make up her mind about the guy she wants to spend the rest of her life with. The male just doesn't like being crowded with female claustrophobia.

. . . but no money gifts for the chicks:
I figure it could be taken the wrong way. Money looks like payment for services rendered, though no one cares a hang if I give a 'broad' a big diamond.

. . . and a thumbs-down reaction to a bevy of chorus girls, hangin' round, and waiting for the come-on signal from The Leader:
I can't stand these broads. They drive me nuts. Let's go to the other room here and listen to Count Basie.

I'm supposed to have a Ph.D. on the subject of women, but the truth is I've funked more often than not. I'm very fond of women; I admire them. But, like all men, I don't understand them.

I crave variety, and I'm delighted when a lady has the imagination to come up with something different. I've never known a woman who could select neckties I really like. I think any gal who could do that, who could pick out a dozen ties I would really like, would pass the supreme test.

I like a woman's clothes to be tasteful and subtle. I don't like excessive make-up. I know that a woman must have a little, but I think that women – generally – have enough beauty without doing the circus tent type make-up. And women who smoke from the moment they open their eyes until they put out the light at night, that drives me batty. It's unfeminine and dangerous – burn up the whole damn house, you know.

WITH JANE RUSSELL

I BELIEVE

The witch doctor tries to convince us that we have to ask God for help, to spell out to Him what we need, even to bribe Him with prayer or cash on the line.

Well, I believe that God knows what each of us wants and needs. It's not necessary for us to make it to church on Sunday to reach Him. You can find Him anywhere. And if that sounds heretical, my source is pretty good: Matthew 5 to 7, the Sermon on the Mount.

There are things about organised religion which I resent. Christ is revered as the Prince of Peace but more blood has been shed in His name than any other figure in history.

Show me one step forward in the name of religion and I'll show you a hundred retrogressions.

Remember, they were men of God who destroyed the educational treasures at Alexandria, who perpetrated the Inquisition in Spain, who burned the witches at Salem.

I detest the two-faced who pretend liberality, but are practised bigots in their own mean little spheres.

I don't tell my daughter whom to marry, but I'd have broken her back if she had had big eyes for a bigot.

As I see it, man is the product of his conditioning. The social forces which mould his morality and conduct—including racial prejudice—are influenced more by material things like good and economic necessities than by the fear and awe and bigotry generated by the high priests of commercialised superstition.

Now, don't get me wrong. I'm for decency— period. I'm for anything and everything that bodes love and consideration for my fellow men. But when lip service to some mysterious deity permits bestiality on Wednesday and absolution on Sunday—count me out.

I've got no quarrel with men of decency at any level. But I can't believe that decency stems

only from religion. And I can't help wondering how many public figures make avowals of faith to maintain an aura of respectability.

Our civilisation, such as it is, was shaped by religion, and the men who aspire to public office any place in the free world must make obeis—ance to God or risk immediate opprobrium.

Have you thought of the chance I'm taking by speaking out this way? Can you imagine the deluge of crank letters, curses, threats and obscenities I'll receive? Worse, the boycott of my records and films.

Why? Because I've dared to say that love and decency are not necessarily concomitants of religious fervour.

Over 25,000 organised religions flourish on this planet, but the followers of each think all the others are miserably misguided and probably evil as well.

In India, they worship white cows, monkeys and dip in the Ganges. The Moslems accept slavery and prepare for Allah, who promises wine and revirginated women.

Remember that leering, cursing lynch mob in Little Rock reviling a meek, innocent little twelve year old Negro girl as she tried to enrol in school? Weren't they—or most of them—devout church-goers?

I'm for anything that gets you through the night, be it prayer, tranquillisers or a bottle of Jack Daniels. But to me religion is a deeply personal thing in which man and God go it alone together without the witch doctor in the middle . . .

KEEPIN' IT IN THE FAMILY
— FOLLOW ME —

SINATRA WITH HIS CHILDREN FRANK AND NANCY SINATRA

Francis, Jr.: Keepin' it in the family . . .
The kid sings better than I did at his stage of development. He's way ahead of me because he's a studied musician, which I am not.

. . . but Papa pulls no punches when Junior doesn't make it . . .
I'm going to kick you right in your francis. Don't ever let me catch you singing like that again, without enthusiasm.

. . . etcetera, etcetera . . .
Get lost! No matter what your name is, you're nothing if you aren't excited about what you're doing.

When my son Frankie said to me he would like to start singing, we came up with the idea of his going with the Dorsey band because it seems to be one of the few that constantly works. In another year, you see, he's going to have the best experience—experience you cannot buy anywhere. He works every single night to a different audience. He learns to understand his lyrics a little better—he's learning now how to execute the song with a little dramatic intent, if necessary, which can lead him into acting. I didn't realise that when I was a young singer, because I never had eyes for anything but being in the music business . . . (1965)

— 74 —

NUCLEAR DISARMAMENT
FEAR...HATE...WAR
— IT'S A BLUE WORLD —

Frank, you're very sick . . .

How can you be against disarmament? After all, despite the universal and unanimous assumption that both Powers—Russia and the United States—already have stockpiled more nuclear weaponry than is necessary to vaporise the entire planet, each Power continues to build, improve and enlarge its terrifying arsenal.

For the first time in history, man has developed the means with which to extinguish all life in one, shuddering instant. And, brother, no one gets a pass, no one hides from this one.

But the question is not so much whether disarmament is desirable or even whether it can be achieved, but whether—if we were able to achieve it—we would be better off, or perhaps infinitely worse off.

I'm a realist, or at least I fancy myself one. Just as I believe that religion doesn't always work, so do I feel that disarmament may be completely beyond man's capacity to live with.

Let's say that somehow the UN is able to achieve total global disarmament. But imagine as well the gnawing doubts, suspicions and nerve-racking tensions which must inevitably begin to fill the void; the fear that the other side—or perhaps some third Power—is secretly arming or still holding a few bombs with which to surprise and overcome the other.

But I firmly believe that nuclear war is absolutely impossible. I don't think anyone in the world wants a nuclear war—not even the Russians. They and we and the Nth countries—as nuclear strategists refer to future nuclear powers—face the incontrovertible certainty of lethal retaliation for any nuclear strike.

I can't believe for a moment that the idiot exists in any nation that will push the first button—not ever accidentally. I know I'm out of my depth when I attempt even to comprehend the complexity of shifting the production of a country from war to peace.

But, if this were to happen, I believe that the deep-seated terror in the hearts of most people due to the constant threat of total destruction would disappear. The result would be a more positive, less greedy, more loving approach to survival.

I can tell you this much from personal experience and observation: hate solves no problems. It only creates them. I was talking the other day to Mike Romanoff (the famous American restaurateur) and I asked him what would happen if a summit meeting of all the leaders in every country in the world was called, including Red China, at the UN.

Further, suppose that each leader brings with him his top aides; Kennedy brings Rusk, Krushchev brings Gromyko, Mao brings Chou. All these cats together in one room, then—boom! Somebody blows up the mother building. No more leaders. No more deputies. The question I asked Mike was, what would happen to the world? I told Mike I thought it might be the only chance the world had for survival. But Mike just shook his head and said: 'Frank, you're very sick'. Maybe so.

Until someone lights the fuse, however, I think that continuation of cold war preparedness might be more effective to maintain the peace than the dewy-eyed notion of total disarmament. I also wonder if 'total' disarmament includes chemical and bacteriological weapons—which, as you know, can be just as lethal as nuclear weapons. I think nuclear testing has got to stop, and I think it will stop—because it has to stop.

Both sides have to live on this planet, and leaders in all countries know that their children and grandchildren have to live here, too. I suspect that when the limits of strontium-90 in the atmosphere get really dangerous, scientists in both camps will persuade the politicians to call a final halt to testing.

Fear is the enemy of logic. There is no more debilitating, crushing, self-defeating, sickening thing in the world. If we continue to fear the Russians, and if they continue to fear us, then we're both in big trouble. Neither side will be able to make logical, reasoned decisions. I think, however, that their fear and concern over the balance of power in some areas is far from irrational.

Our concern over a Sovietised Cuba, for instance, must be equated with Russian concern over our missile bases surrounding them. It is proper that we should be concerned but we must see their side of the coin—and not let this concern turn into fear on either side.

THE COMMIES
— ANYTIME, ANYWHERE —

It strikes me that we should stop worrrying about Communism—instead, we should get rid of the conditions that nurture it. I think that Communism can fester only wherever and whenever it is encouraged to breed.

Poverty is probably the greatest asset the Communists have. Wherever it exists, any place in the world, you have a potential Communist breeding ground.

It figures that if a man is frustrated in a material sense, his family hungry, then be broods and he becomes susceptible to the blandishments of any ideology that promises to take him off the hook.

Hunger is inexcusable in a world where grain rots in silos and butter turns rancid while being held for favourable trade conditions.

A lot of us consider the UN a private club—ours, of course—with gentlemen's agreements just like any other exclusive club. But instead of excluding a person, a race or religion, the members of the UN have the power to exclude entire nations. I don't happen to think you can kick 800,000,000 Chinese under the carpet and simply pretend they don't exist. Because they do.

If the UN doesn't represent the united nations of the world, then what the hell have you got? Not democracy – and certainly not world government.

Speaking just as an ordinary guy who thinks and worries, I believe that if we can stay out of war for the next ten years, we'll never have another war. From all I've read and seen recently, I'm betting that within the next decade the Russians are going to want colour TV, their wives are going to want electrified kitchens, their kids are going to want hot rods.

Even Russian girls are getting hip; I've seen photos of them at Russian beach resorts, and it looks like the Riviera. They're thinning down, and I see they're going the bikini route. It means the girls are interested in being girls and the boys are going to stop thinking about communes and begin thinking connubially.

You know, I'd love to visit Russia, and sometime later, China too. I figure the more I know about them the more they know about me, the better chance we have of living in peace.

I'd love to go and show them American music. I'd take Count Basie and Ella Fitzgerald and

we'd do what we do best. I'm betting that they'd dig us. That's got to create some kind of goodwill – and man a little goodwill is something we could use.

I think we can make it if we live and let live. And love one another – I mean really love. If you don't know the guy on the other side of the world, love him anyway because he's just like you. He has the same dreams, the same hopes and fears. It's one world, pal. We're all neighbours.

But didn't somebody once go up on to a mountain long ago and say the same thing to the world?

BIGOTRY

— PLEASE BE KIND —

I've been up and down America a lot since I first started singing and I've seen a lot to make me feel both proud and ashamed of being an American. I've seen racial and religious intolerance take all kinds of forms and many times I've seen one man's hand raised against his brother simply because he didn't like the colour of his skin.

I have also seen decency and sanity rise out of the depths of depression and fear, and assert themselves in truly wonderful ways. It is not my task to preach to anyone or sell social messages to my fellow citizens but I happen to hold a few convictions about life and democracy.

I hold certain definite opinions about some of the problems currently dividing our nation and frequently I feel the urge to express myself, to speak out on issues that entertainers don't normally concern themselves with.

I believe that an entertainer's function is to entertain. But he is also a responsible citizen with the same rights and obligations as the next man. When an entertainer shirks his duty as a citizen in a crisis, he is as much to be criticised as anybody else. And when he faces up courageously to an issue which, because of its national importance, affects him directly, he is entitled to applause.

Louis Armstrong, whom I've long admired for his artistry, faced up to a great national issue last September and sounded off strongly in an interview given to a newspaperman in Grand Forks, N.D. Louis was understandably angry over the failure of the federal government to act quickly and firmly to protect the right of nine Negro students to go to a high school in Little Rock without being segregated. A lot of people sided with Armstrong on that deal. Others said he was too outspoken and should not make statements outside the area of music.

Though I felt at the time that Pops might have left out a few words about his President and government, I believe he was basically right and perfectly justified in saying what he did. His was a righteous indignation over injustice.

It has been much more than a long association. I have been on the receiving end of inspiration from a succession of great Negro singers and jazz artists stretching all the way back to early Louis Armstrong and Duke Ellington—who is happily at last recognised as one of his country's most distinguished composers.

When Nat Cole was assaulted on a theatre stage by bigoted hoodlums in Birmingham, Alabama, the whole entertainment profession experienced a sense of outrage. I was furious when I heard of the incident and immediately tried to reach Nat by phone to see how he was feeling, and to tell him of my own personal anger at what had happened.

I finally reached him in a motel on the road at 3am the following morning, and conveyed my concern and sympathy. I simply said I was shocked, sorry and angry over the outrage. Nat is not only a great entertainer but a first-rate citizen, a very classy gentleman who honours his profession wherever he appears. I am proud to count him as a friend.

I have a lot of friends in show business and they come from all walks of life and represent almost every imaginable skin tint. Professionally and musically, I can't begin to fully evaluate the tremendous importance of Negro singers and musicians to my development as a singer. The debt I owe them is too immense ever to be repaid.

On the question of bigots and bigotry, Sinatra says that the intellectual is often:
. . . twice as dangerous as the person with no education. The uneducated man can be taught he is wrong. But the intellectual will rationalise.

PRIDE & PREJUDICE
— I SHOULD CARE —

There's no point in going around calling other kids names or indicating your racial prejudices.

The children themselves are not to blame for religious and racial intolerance. It's the parents . . . Kids hear their parents talking about the McGintys or the Ginsbergs and then think there must be something awfully wrong with being a Catholic or a Jew . . . No child is born bad. If parents were less selfish and took the time to teach their children that there is something else in the world besides greed and hate, we'd have a better world . . .

This prejudice, it's nothing new to me. In Hoboken when I was a kid and somebody called me a 'dirty little Guinea', there was only one thing to do—break his head. After I got older, I realised you've got to do it through education.

Back then, I used to feel an indignity that shook me up. But I know that you don't lick that sort of thing overnight.

SINATRA AND THE MOB
— NOTHING IN COMMON —

On the press allegations that he met Lucky Luciano and other leading Mafia mobsters in Havana, '47:
What actually happened is that in 1947 I had some time off and decided to vacation in Havana and Mexico City. On the way, I stopped off at Miami to play a benefit for the Damon Runyon Cancer Fund. I ran into Joe Fischetti there and when he found I was headed for Havana, he told me he and his brothers were going, too. He changed his reservation to be on my plane . . .

That night, I was having a drink at the bar with Connie Immerman, a New York restaurateur, and met a large group of men and women. As so often happens in big groups, the introductions were perfunctory. I was invited to have dinner with them, and while dining I realised that one of the men in the party was Lucky Luciano. It suddenly struck me that I was laying myself open to criticism by remaining at the table, but I could think of no way to leave in the middle of dinner without creating a scene.

After dinner I went to the jai alai games and then with an acquaintance, toured the night spots. We finally wound up at the Havana Casino where we passed a table at which were Luciano and several other men. They insisted that we sit down for a drink. Again, rather than cause a disturbance, I had a quick drink and excused myself. These were the only times I've ever seen Luciano in my life.

. . . and to a further allegation that he conveyed $2,000,000 in small bills to Luciano . . . :
Picture me, skinny Frankie, lifting $2,000,000 in small bills. For the record $1,000 in dollar bills weighs three pounds which makes the load I am supposed to have carried 6,000 pounds. Even assuming that the bills were $20s—the bag would still have required a couple of stevedores to carry it. This is probably the most ridiculous charge that has ever been levelled at me . . . I stepped off the plane in Havana with a small bag in which I carried my oils, sketching material and personal jewellery, which I never send with my regular luggage.

. . . and to yet another allegation about his association with more hoods . . .
I was brought up to shake a man's hand when I am introduced to him without first investigating his past. Any report that I fraternised with goons or racketeers is a vicious lie.

As for the remarks attributed to me relative to the mob, they're strictly out of a comic strip. I don't make threats, and I'm not running for re-election.

Some things I can't ever talk about. Someone might come knockin' at my . . . door.

It's true that this is a country born of violence. But what's happening is frightening, and frankly, I don't know how it's going to end. I don't feel that these people really know what they want.

Sure, I knew some of those guys. I spent a lot of time working in saloons. And saloons are not

run by Christian Brothers. I didn't meet any Nobel prize winners in saloons. But if Francis of Assisi was a singer, he would've met the same guys.

That doesn't make them part of something. They said hello, you said hello. They came backstage. They thanked you. You offered them a drink. That was it. And it doesn't matter any more, does it? Most of the guys I knew, or met, are dead.

SINATRA V THE PRESS
— YOU'RE DRIVING ME CRAZY —

His treatment, generally, by the press?
It's been shitty. There's no other word for it. A bunch of lies. From time to time in the entertainment business, somebody comes along who says to the press, after maltreatment for a specific amount of time, 'Don't bother me any more! I don't need you'. They have, of course, resented it. People in the press from time to time have acted like they have the privilege of a god. I got my brains knocked out. Fifteen years ago I said I wasn't going to talk to the press any more. It became an undeclared war. There has to be a scapegoat. I guess I'm one of them.

All alone:
'But an artist in the public eye should realise that he has no private life', you say? Nonsense. Everyone's entitled to a degree of privacy — I don't care who he is.

To a photographer, determined to get his own shots of the Sinatra-Ava Gardner wedding (1951):
I'll bet you fifty dollars you don't get a picture and another fifty dollars that if you even point your camera at me, I'll knock you on the ear.

... and a word or two for Australian newsmen, at Melbourne Stadium, re possibility of get-together of divorcees, Frank and Ava (1959):
If I see you again you'll never forget it. If you're around later, they'll find you in the gutter.

The German Press, by FS, Albert Hall, 1975:
A funny thing happened on the way to Berlin the other day, he confided to a packed Royal

Albert Hall. All we wanted to do there was to sing some songs — but they called me a super-gangster, whatever that can mean?

Capone wasn't a super-gangster. I'm not a super-gangster or any kind of gangster. I don't understand the German press. I haven't done anything to them. I even say Gesundheit! (God Bless you!) when I sneeze.

I was disappointed. I'm a professional entertainer and a lot of people wanted to see us and couldn't. I don't care about their damn press — what's it anyway? — but I could have retorted and started to make remarks about their forefathers. I could have started mentioning something about the sins of the fathers ... like Dachau and a few places like that ... if they want to start calling me a super-gangster.

I don't know why they do this to me. I love Germany. I've even got a German car. At least I think it's German. It's got power-steering, power brakes, everything's power.

DONCHA' GO 'WAY MAD

Strictly for the Press
... a telegram to a House Judiciary Committee,
investigating the US TV industry, in respect of
an old foe, from Columbia Records days:
Before Mitch Miller's arrival at Columbia, I
found myself enjoying a freedom of selection of
material, a freedom which I may modestly say
resulted in a modicum of success for me.
Suddenly Mr Miller, by design or coincidence,
began to present many inferior songs, all
curiously bearing the BMI label (Broadcast
Music, Inc). Before Mr Miller's advent on the
scene, I had a successful recording career which
quickly went into decline. Rather than
continue a frustrating battle, I choose to take
my talents elsewhere. It is now a matter of
record that since I have associated myself with
Capitol Records, a company free of
broadcasting affiliations, my career is again
financially, creatively and artistically healthy.

A greetings telegram for Clifford Davis
following the 'Daily Mirror' TV editor's report
that Sinatra was not present for his Festival
Hall concert rehearsal:
Since you seem to show such interest in my
activities, why the hell don't you bother to find
out that I wasn't supposed to be there—repeat
wasn't supposed to be there. Irresponsible
journalism stinks. Sinatra.

... Sinatra's reply to member of the Tommy
Dorsey band, who said he'd never get a good
write-up from a drunken journalist he'd
dumped on his francis for making an anti-
Semitic remark:
If my career depended on prejudiced guys like
that I'd forget it.

... an in-person acknowledgement to an absent
'friend' ...:
Dot Kilgallen isn't here. She's out shopping for
a new chin.

... riposte to David Susskind, US TV
impresario, who had rejected, sarcastically,
Sinatra's proposed fee of $250,000 for an
'Open End' discussion of Sinatra and The
Clan:
The $250,000 fee is for my usual talent of song
and dance. However, now that I understand
the picture a little more clearly, I must change it

to $750,000 for all parasitical programmes.

Memo to a 'Los Angeles Daily News'
columnist:
Just continue to print lies about me and my
temper—not my temperament. Will see that
you get a belt in your stupid and vicious mouth.
(1946)

... an invasion of privacy suit against the
publishers of 'Look' magazine, December
1957:
I have always maintained that any writer or
publication has a right to discuss or criticise my
professional activities as a singer or actor. But I
feel that an entertainer's right to privacy should
be just as inviolate as any other person's right to
privacy.

SINATRA AND THE PRESS
— I'VE GOT YOU UNDER MY SKIN —

All day long they lie in the sun. And after the
sun goes down, they lie some more.

A few well-chosen words of greeting to
'Washington Post' columnist Maxine
Cheshire:
Get away from me. You scum, go home and
take a bath. Print that, Miss Cheshire. Get

away from me. I don't want to talk to you. I'm getting out of here to get rid of the stench of Miss Cheshire . . . You know Miss Cheshire, don't you? That stench you smell is from her . . . you're a – – – –, that's spelled – – – –. You know what that means, don't you? . . . here's two dollars, baby. That's what you're used to . .

An altercation between FS, and an unnamed reporter (who asked him his future plans) . . .
You newspaper men are all a bunch of – – – – –s . . .
and a photographer called Finkelstein . . .
Run the – – – – – down. Kill the no-good – – – – – . . .

Okay. But did you really try suicide . . .?
I've never heard of anything so damn wild and ridiculous. This would be a hell of a time to do away with myself. I've been trying to lick this thing for two years and I've practically got it

licked now. I did not try to commit suicide. I just had a bellyache. What will you guys think of next to write about me?

Tuesday night, Miss Gardner, my manager Hank Sanicola and Mrs Sanicola dined at the Christmas Tree Inn on Lake Tahoe. Ava was returning to Hollywood that night. We came back to the Lake and I didn't feel so good. So I took two sleeping pills. Miss Gardner left by auto for Reno and the plane trip back to Hollywood. By now it was early Wednesday morning. I guess I wasn't thinking because I am very allergic to sleeping pills. Also, I had drunk two or three brandies. I broke out in a rash. The pills felt kind of stuck in my chest. I got worried and called a friend who runs the steak house here. He sent a doctor who gave me a glass of warm water with salt in it. It made me throw up and I was all right. That's all there was to it – honest.

I GET ALONG WITHOUT YOU VERY WELL

Dear Louella Parsons . . .
I'll begin by saying that if you care to make a bet, I'll be glad to take your money that MGM and Frank Sinatra do not part company, permanently or otherwise. Secondly, Frankie has not been a very difficult boy on the lot. Frankie has only been heard from when it concerns the improvement of the picture, which you will find happens in most pictures where you use human beings. Your article claims my pout was caused by something about a song.

Regardless of where you got this information, from some gossip-monger or otherwise, you can rest assured that if I pouted at all, it would have been for a much bigger reason than a broken-down song. As an added thought, I have always been one of the most stalwart defenders of the phrase 'nobody is indispensable', so your line about my being irreplaceable was all wet. Last but not least, in the future I'll appreciate your not wasting your breath in any lectures because when I feel I need one I'll seek such advice from someone who either writes or tells the truth. You have my permission to print this if you desire and clear up a great injustice. Frank Sinatra. (1947)

. . . and a musical explanation for yet another brawl . . .
It was just one of those things.

A statement that surprised many, following action by Nevada Gaming Control Board to revoke Sinatra's gaming licence following allegations that he had entertained Mafia heavy Sam Giancana as his guest at the Cal-Neva Lodge, July '63 . . . :
No useful purpose would be served by my devoting my time and energies convincing the Nevada gaming officials that I should be part of their industry.

PRESS UPS (AND DOWNS)

— I'M NOT AFRAID —

My bête noire, Lee Mortimer. All I did was nod a greeting across the room when I spotted him. And then it started . . . He gave me a look. I can't describe it. It was one of those 'Who do you amount to?' looks. I followed him out. I hit him. I'm all mixed up.
(1947)

. . . and there was that driving incident involving the airport photographer . . .
I admit I was mad. I figured the crippled photographer was planted there just to get me to take a swing at him. I slammed my foot on the gas without realising the wheels were turned. The car swerved before I could straighten it. I'm sorry.

This guy, Al Aronowitz of the 'New York Post', 'phoned about daughter Nancy's wedding to Tommy Sands . . . And I told Al, I said:
I just want to know where you got the − − − to call me after what you write about me (in 1959). I'm not going to tell you a thing. You're a cop and you're a fink and you're a parasite. I've got $3,000,000, Al, and I don't need you. You can bleed, Al, because I'll never tell you anything, you fink.

After 'Time' had reported I was about to buy a Palm Beach pad and night-club, so I could wage a war with an established night-club owner who had refused me $5,000 for a one-shot appearance, I sent this telegram . . .:
I am glad to see that you are still batting a thousand regarding any information concerning me. As usual your information stinks. I need a house and a night-club in Palm Beach like you need a tumour.

THE FIRST COMEBACK

— I'VE GOT THE WORLD ON A STRING —

So, like I say, it was a low year. Then I realised I was pushing forty, so one day I got up and just decided to go to work.

I wanted to start again with a clean slate. I changed my agent and I changed my record company. That was a big help, I guess.

My voice, that's still the same. The stuff I recorded maybe had a lot to do with it. I had a lot of good songs.

I'LL REMEMBER MAGGIO
MEMORIES OF THE FILM
— OH! LOOK AT ME NOW —

'From Here To Eternity':
I was working with the finest pros. I felt like I was playing with the Yankees and I knew it was going well. I learned from all of them. But Montgomery Clift was particularly helpful . . . The way he pitched, I couldn't help shining as a catcher.

You know, there's one thing I wanted to say when I accepted the Oscar for 'From Here To Eternity'. I wanted to thank Monty Clift personally. I learned more about acting from Clift – well, it was equal to what I learned about musicals from Gene Kelly.

Such great helpers, Clift and Burt Lancaster, the both:
They helped me a lot in that picture. They're both such great guys and great actors. They just about lived their parts, because they knew them so well and they helped me make what I did out of mine.

FROM HERE TO POSTERITY

— ALL OR NOTHING AT ALL —

When I first saw the script I just knew I had to play Maggio. I wanted it badly. That guy was me. I needed the money but I wanted to be Maggio so bad that I'd have worked free.

For the first time in my life I was reading something I really had to do. I just felt it—I just knew I could do it, and I just couldn't get it out of my head. I knew that if a picture was ever made, I was the only actor to play Private Maggio, the funny and sour Italo-American. I knew Maggio. I went to high school with him in Hoboken. I was beaten up with him. I might have been Maggio.

A fervent plea to producer Buddy Adler:
It's me, I've got to have it. Buddy, I've never asked you for anything before. But I'm ready to beg. Give me the part and you'll never be sorry.

. . . followed by a passionate ask of Harry Cohn, Columbia Pictures boss:
It was written for me—for me and nobody else. I'm not kidding, Harry, but you can get your Maggio for—a thousand a week.

An airline trip from Africa—and Ava—for the screen test:
I caught the next plane to Hollywood. For the test, I played the saloon scene where Maggio shakes the dice with the olives and the scene where he's found drunk outside the Royal Hawaiian Hotel. I was scared to death. The next day I flew back to Africa, probably the longest route an actor ever travelled for a fifteen-minute screen test . . .

. . . and later, after getting the part:
Now, I'll show all those wise guys! I'll show all those mothers!

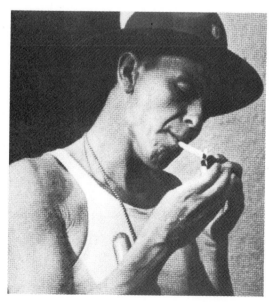

LET'S FACE THE MUSIC AND...

'PAL JOEY'—The True-Life Musical

Hollywood has finally made a musical without most of the inevitable clichés that go with such a film.

I don't sit at the piano in a striped silk shirt with arm garters, as the customers yell for another chorus of 'Piano-roll Blues'. I didn't have any accidents in which I lose my voice, with the doctor sadly telling me that I'll never sing again.

There isn't any haunting of music firms, begging an agent to publish one of our songs—a surefire hit written because of my great love for my girlfriend. We didn't open the picture in a cellar saloon, with sawdust on the floor and waiters with handlebar moustaches running around with trays held high over their vaseline-slick heads, doing a soft-shoe number between drinks.

And the biggest agent in New York doesn't have his car break down in front of the night club, stroll in for a beer, listen in amazement to my song, drop a contract in my lap and say: 'There's room for you but not your girlfriend'. In fact, 'Pal Joey' ends the same way as it begins—with me out of a job.

Joey Evans pleases Columbia chief over billing teaser . . .

We talked things out and then I saw an uneasy look coming into the faces of the Cohn braintrust and Harry himself. I don't like frightened people and I don't like being frightened myself. So I asked, 'What's the trouble?'. All were afraid to talk up. 'If it's billing', I said, 'it's okay to make it Hayworth/Sinatra/Novak. I don't mind being in the middle of that sandwich. Man, were they relieved!

'OCEAN'S ELEVEN'

We've been making a movie here—it's about a guy named Danny Ocean, whose eleven pals plan a ten million dollar robbery in five big gambling casinos. The way the script is going—I think we should forget the picture and pull the job . . .!

Well, it's a pretty far cry from 'Guys & Dolls' but it's a part I've had my heart on for a long, long time. John Garfield first wanted to do it, and after he died I tried to buy the book. It doesn't matter that I didn't get it; all that matters is, after all these years of waiting, I get to play the part.

FILMS BY FRANK

Whaddabout your own favourite movies, Frank . . .?
Oh, all of them I like. 'The Tender Trap' was a lot of fun to do. I enjoyed working with Doris Day in 'Young At Heart', and, of course, there was 'The Man With The Golden Arm'. That part was a kind of challenge. I really studied for it, y'know? Spent a lot of time with doctors, watching guys in dope clinics and all that.

Let's face it, some of your movies—like 'Sergeants Three', ain't all that hot . . .!
Of course they're not great movies. No one could claim that. But every movie I've made through my own company has made money, and it's not so easy to say that. 'Ocean's Eleven' has grossed millions of dollars, and 'Sergeants Three' is already well on the way to doing the same. 'Manchurian Candidate' could make a lot of money, too—it could be a great movie. The whole business of making movies fascinates me. But the movie business is in a very bad state, and I hate to see it that way. I would love to do anything in my power to rectify the situation.

FRANK SINATRA WITH DEBBIE REYNOLDS

The real necessity is to make good movies that make money—and recently that just has not been done. The way I see it is that Pay-TV has got to come. It would give the film industry a terrific shot in the arm. I can see us making one picture a year, taking six months to do it, doing it really properly. Spend ten or fifteen million dollars on it, lavish as you can make it. But it's got to be a good product as well as lavish, of course. Then you show it on colour TV to forty million people at, say, fifty cents a head. Do that three times—pow pow pow—and you're really in business.

The greatest change in my life began the night they gave me an Oscar. It's funny about that statue. You walk up on the stage like you are in a dream and they hand you that little man before twenty or thirty million people and you have to fight to keep the tears back. It's a moment. Like your first girl or your first kiss. Like the first time you hit a guy and he went down. I've heard actors kid about the Academy Awards. Don't believe them. It was a big moment in their lives.

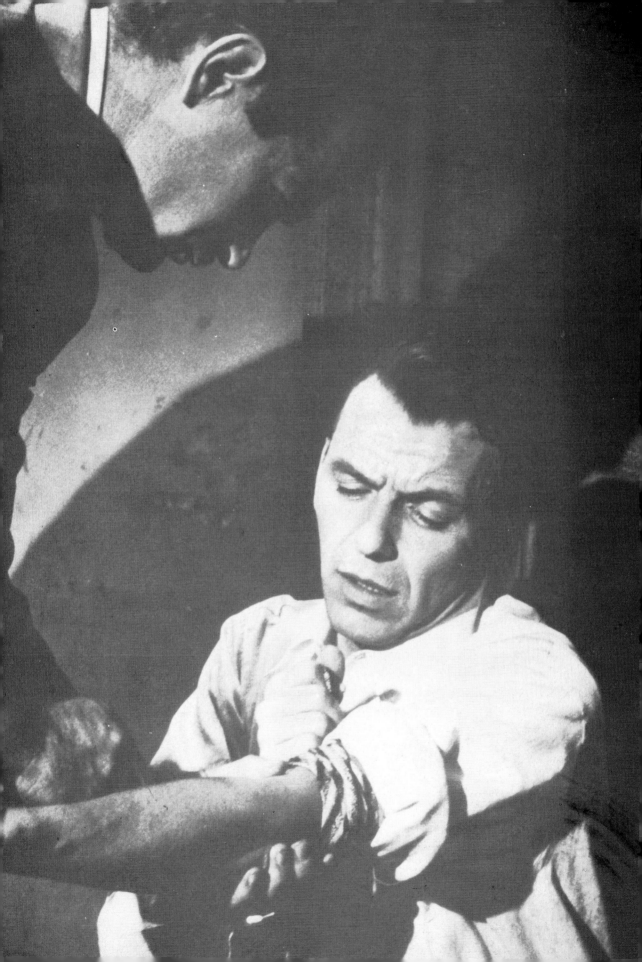

MOVIE MOMENTS
— THERE ARE SUCH THINGS —

How did FS think cinema audiences would react to the situation in 'KINGS GO FORTH' where white soldier marries black girl?:
I think most people who have any kind of common sense and think fairly will not go out of the theatre and start race riots. As for the bigots, they'll scream at anything. But I took this part as a performer, not as a lecturer on racial problems.

Sinatra as Joe E. Lewis in 'THE JOKER IS WILD':
Joe was a helluva singer before the punks heeled on him. Everybody who knew him then (when a Chicago café owner ordered him killed rather than let him go to a competitor), said he really had a voice. I wouldn't play just a singer in a movie—like a Russ Columbo or a Rudy Vallee. Joe's is a powerful story.

SINATRA AND MITZI GAYNOR

'THE PRIDE & THE PASSION' (and Seen-yor
See-natra)
I engaged a guitarist Vicente Gomez. I gave him
the script of 'The Pride', put him into a
recording studio and had him read all my lines.
I want to play this role like a Spaniard trying to
speak English – not like an American trying to
talk like a Spaniard trying to speak English.

'CAN – CAN' (but this time, François is from
Hoboken, would yer know!)
Originally, I was to play the role of François, a
playboy lawyer, with a French accent. Shirley
MacLaine politely reminded me of the last time
I tried an accent – in a Technicolor wide-screen
epic called 'The Pride and the Passion' in which
I played a Spanish Guerilla with bangs and
which I'd like to forget.

I realised the girl had a point. François is being
played straight – or at least as straight as I can
play him.

SINATRA & THE SILVER SCREEN

— I'M GONNA MAKE IT ALL THE WAY —

I always try to remember three things as a movie actor. First, you must know why you are in a movie, understand all the reactions of the man you are playing, figure out why he's doing what he is doing. Secondly, you must know the script. Some actors are crammers—they cram the night before and just learn their lines the following day. I don't do it that way. I keep a script in my office, my car, my bedroom, by the telephone, even in the john. And I read the whole script maybe fifty or sixty times before shooting even starts. Then, when it comes to shooting a particular scene, you just have to glance at the script to remember the lines and, more important, you know how that scene fits into the picture as a whole.

Thirdly, you must learn and listen to the lines of others; it's no good just learning your own. With Spencer Tracy, for instance, you don't get time between his lines and yours to think out your next. There's only one thing about making movies that really irritates me: this business of overdubbing songs to the vision afterwards. With all the advance in

microphone equipment you'd think they could have worked out some way of recording at the same time as filming. I never sing a song exactly the same way twice, so when I come to mime I find it very hard. Somehow miming seems to take away a lot of the spontaneity, and I find myself unconsciously thinking of different ways I might sing the song.

If a movie-goer spends five shillings to see me in a motion picture, he has the right to see me at my best. I do not feel, however, that I have any responsibility to that movie-goer to tell him anything about my private life.

I try to take a leaf out of Marlon Brando's book when I get a film part. I try to analyse any part I play. I study people all the time just in case I have to play someone like them.

F.S. on 'THE MANCHURIAN CANDIDATE':

I'm more excited about this part than any other part I've played. I'm saying kinds of things in this script that I've never had to speak on the

FRANK SINATRA WITH LAURENCE HARVEY

screen before. Never had to speak at all, for that matter. Long wild speeches. For instance, my first words in the film are a long speech about the different note value systems on the clarinet. Sometimes before I've even ad-libbed for three whole pages of script, just been myself talking as I would do normally. But this is different. Very, very different.

This is without doubt the finest picture I have ever made, but I don't know what to say when people ask me what it's about, other than to tell them that every night while making the picture I stayed up, worrying about the part.

'THE HOUSE I LIVE IN'

You can't beat the kids on the head with eloquence and fancy words. You have to talk to them in their own language.

It's a funny part. I've been looking for a comedy for some time. I read the book five years ago, and wondered whether anybody would ever do it. When I read the script, I said, 'I've read this before'.

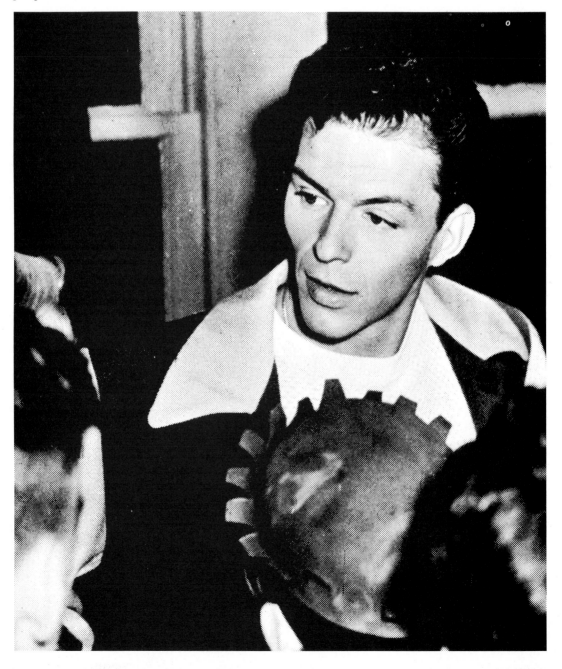

EVERYTHING HAPPENS TO ME

What about the first attempt at acting and directing a film—'None But The Brave' . . .?
I found out that it was in some ways tougher than I had thought. The director has so many things to worry about—pace, wardrobe, the performances . . . Next time I won't try to perform when I direct . . .

. . . and what about those second-rate films?:
I guess the trouble has been that at the time nothing better seemed to be available. It all boils down to material.

. . . a moot point about film-making—one that involves technique plus finance . . .
Musicians play on a sound stage for a movie. You can't use their work on records without paying them again. Why should an actor make two films for the price of one? I'm not talking about the use of two cameras. They can shoot any scene with as many cameras as they want—and they do. I'm talking about playing the same scene twice.

. . . and another matter of financial recompense—this time re a proposed appearance on the Ed Sullivan Show:
It is not fair to do a show for Sullivan with no pay and then in the same breath ask others to pay me . . . I turned down Sullivan for a similar free shot with 'Not As A Stranger'. They can

use film clips. But when you make a special appearance, you're entitled to compensation. If it's a TV trailer for Goldwyn who bought the airtime, I'd do it. I told Goldwyn if my schedule allows, I'll be glad to do personal appearances to help promote the picture when it's released. I told Goldwyn I'd work on the Sullivan Show if Sullivan paid and gave the money to charity.

I know there are singers who work on melody primarily, who get a big deal of melodic sounds going for them. Opera is something else. Even opera singers I've talked to admit they don't worry about enunciation, even in a foreign tongue. What they're worrying about is tonal quality. That's what their racket is all about. I'm a lyric singer.

I'm crazy about strings for a vocal background. Maybe I'd never have left Harry James if he had had strings at the time I was with him.

It's terribly difficult to remain completely stable when you suddenly zoom from no place to where you're constantly surrounded by people pulling you in several directions. The money is always there . . . although you really don't know how much is there. Soon you get confused and you don't care . . . Every time I felt insecure, I used to go out and buy ten more suits.

SINATRA & MOVIE-MAKING
— YOU CAN TAKE MY WORD FOR IT BABY —

A kinda untimely remark?:
Pictures stink. Most of the people in them do, too. I don't want any more movie acting. Hollywood won't believe I'm through, but they'll find out I mean it.

Film stars came in for a stinging slap:
It's a good thing not any of these jerks came up as rapidly as I did. If they had, you couldn't get near them without running interference through three secretaries.

How can I possibly play a love scene at nine in the morning? Not me! I work better later in the day. That's why I only record at night. But nobody wanted to break the precedent about filming in the evening—until I did with an independent production.

A Sinatra reaction to the House Un-American Activities Committee investigation of the US film industry:
Once they get the movies throttled, how long will it be before the Committee gets to work on freedom of the air . . . If you make a pitch on a nation-wide network for a square deal for the underdog, will they call you a commie? (1947)

. . . but hear this, brother:
Now, wouldn't I be a sucker to shoot off like that? Hollywood and the picture people have been good to me. Sure, I'm going to stay in pictures. That is, as long as they want me. But for those things the paper quoted me as saying, I was downright amazed when they showed me the clipping. I couldn't believe that such a story could be made of some reporter's imagination.

. . . or as MGM's press department put it:
It's easy for a guy to get hot under the collar. Literally and figuratively, when he's dressed in a hot suit of navy blue and the temperature is 104° and he's getting over a cold to boot. I think I might have spoken too broadly about quitting pictures and about my feeling towards Hollywood. I'm still under a seven year contract to RKO, which has six years to run. I have one more commitment at Metro following 'Anchors Aweigh' and believe me I intend to live up to my contractual obligations.

Mind you, if you want the real story . . .:
I never made that statement . . . My friends in Hollywood know me too well to believe that I'd ever be that kind of ingrate. I'm too fond of Hollywood and the people who live there.

RETIREMENT
— GOODBYE? —

*For over three decades I have had the great and good fortune to enjoy a rich and rewarding and deeply satisfying career as an entertainer and public figure.

If I gave up performing tomorrow, I would not miss it for five minutes. No, I wouldn't. I get my elation now out of management – giving people jobs, making suggestions, seeing them worked out . . . (1963)

Hell, I just quit, that's all. I don't want to put on any more make-up. I don't want to perform any more. I'm tired. I want to relax and do absolutely zero . . .

I probably won't write a book. If I did, it wouldn't be one of those 'and then I did' kind of books . . .

Retiring because he's dying?
My health is spectacular. In fact, it's never been better. That's why those goddam rumours burn me so. It shows the irresponsibility of the American press . . .

*The official personal farewell – 13 June 1971.

SINATRA AND ROSALIND RUSSELL

Since those two events (retirement and comeback) came so close you must wonder why I gave it all up.

Well, it seemed like a good idea . . . to loaf and play golf. After several years, I have a 17 handicap. And the other day I made an overseas call and the operator asked me how to spell my name. I told her . . . and she asked my first name. Then she said: 'Junior?'

I didn't find retirement all that I expected it to be. I was under constant pressure to return to work.

I'm returning to show business on my own terms.

BETWEEN YOU AND ME
— I'M GONNA LIVE TILL I DIE —

Dying is a pain in the ass . . .

The public knows what it wants and it's up to the record company and the entertainer to deliver.

Welcome sign at Sinatra dwelling—Coldwater Canyon:
If you haven't been invited, you better have a damn good reason for ringing this bell.

I Concentrate On You: good advice for the in-person vocal entertainers everywhere:
Concentrate. Concentrate on the music, on the people around you. Every song holds a special meaning for someone and you can't think of yourself.

Your autograph, Mr Sinatra, please . . .
It's a funny thing. They never come out and ask for an autograph direct—for themselves, I mean. It's always for their kid or their niece. I guess they're embarrassed.

Temperament went out with high-button shoes.
CLAN—WHAT CLAN . . .?
It's a figment of someone's imagination. Naturally people in Hollywood socialise with friends, as they do in any community. But we do not get together in childish fraternities, as some people would like to think.

THE SECOND COMEBACK
— THE SECOND TIME AROUND —

Feel like I haven't worked in years.

I kept getting mail from people who wanted to hear me sing again. There was something like 30,000 letters, and many of them sympathised with my desire for privacy. But they suggested that there were ways I could perform again without sacrificing my private life.

Members of my own organisation have been trying to convince me to make a return. My family, too. So I decided I would go back to work, but only when I could control the situation.

. . . more gigs for the people?
Only when I can control the situation. I'm not going to put myself in the position of facing big, uncontrolled crowds again. Too many times I became the victim in such situations, and I'm not going to let that happen again.

THE WORLD OF MUSIC
— ANYTHING GOES —

Music—Country Style . . .
There's a lot of good music being written in that vein. I'm doing an album myself so I guess the old dog will be learning a few new tricks.

I was talking to Nancy about tunes and she said to me, 'Daddy, why don't you do some Country' and I said, 'I'd like to do some Country but we haven't found anything, and she said, 'Why don't you get a hold of Snuffy?'. And I said, 'All right we'll do that' and that's how it started . . . it's that simple.

I've done Country before years ago but with what I've been doing with Gordon Jenkins and the big goddam orchestras, this is now a whole different world and I like it.

Stylistic question: If your recording of 'The Only Couple On The Floor' is so Country-based, can you call it a Country release . . .?
If it comes out that way I think we should say that. There's no sense in disguising it. A song's a song to me. I don't care what the hell it is. If it's something I can do, I'll do it. I don't think you can force a song into anything. You can't make something that's pop a Country.

So, Frank, how about you doing a Broadway musical sometime, asked Richard Rodgers . . .:
I'd probably want to leave a week after the opening.

. . . okay, but how does acid rock grab you . . .?
I can't hear it. I don't understand anything they're saying. I know that it has a reason, I understand all that. I like all music. I am an opera buff, symphony buff and I think the more serious writers are getting better and better. Paul Williams and those guys—Webb is beginning to write again—they're fabulous writers.

I'M IN THE MONEY

— MISTER SUCCESS —

There's no biz-ness like dough biz-ness . . .
I'm lucky because I have good people working
for me. I wouldn't trust my own judgement
without advice from people who've worked
among financial and business problems all
their lives. Hire the right people – that's the
trick. Eventually I want to be less and less the
public entertainer and more and more in the
background. As a singer I'll only have a few
more years to go – as an actor maybe a few
more than that but not many. I've been
performing out front for nearly thirty years
now and frankly I'm getting a bit tired. Now I
want to do more and more behind the scenes,
using my head. Finance fascinates me.

When I think of myself five years hence I see
myself not so much an entertainer as a high-
level executive, interested in business, perhaps
in directing and producing films . . . The things
I'm involved in personally – such as acting and
recording – steadily earn less money while the
things I have going for me earn most. And
that's the way I want it to be.

Eventually, I want to be less and less before the
public and more and more in the background.
I'll be forty-seven years old in December. I
won't really have had it but, you know, when I
get around that age there's not much I'll want
to play or could play.

Frankly, I'm fascinated with finances. I've been
performing thirty years now and I'm getting a
little lazy about this kind of work. I'd like to
have something working for me for a change.
But I'm narrowing the field of investments to
show business. That interests me. I'm part of it.
Anything else bores me and what bores me
loses me.

I consider myself a fair administrator and
executive. But I have a big staff (at that time
there were thirty executives and professional
advisers in Sinatra's organisation) because I
wouldn't trust my own judgement without
competent advice. The real trick is to get the
right people and I've been fortunate.

There's an excitement about managing a
business that gives as much of a kick as playing
in a film.

AMONG MY SOUVENIRS

Pitching for FDR . . .
My first real criticism from the press came when I campaigned for President Roosevelt in 1944. A few columnists took me to task, insisting that entertainers should stick to entertaining. Most stars agree with this. They also realise it is bad public relations to indulge in politics because you may lose fans who don't agree with you. However, I feel it is the duty of every American citizen to help elect the candidate of his choice. Ginger Rogers, George Murphy and other stars supported Tom Dewey during this campaign, and I noted that none of my critics lambasted them.

. . . and others, later . . .
If I want to have my say as a citizen, and doing it is going to hurt me in show business then I say to hell with show business.

I don't want these meetings ballyhooed like a show. When I go some place to talk, I'm Frank Sinatra, citizen, not an entertainer.

It is my proudest possession.
. . . a framed, signed photograph of JFK, inscribed: 'For Frank, with the warm regards and best wishes of his friend, Jack Kennedy'

. . . and some showbiz contributions to JFK Presidential election drive in happier times:
We expect to raise 1,700,000 dollars for the one night. This is something that hasn't been done before. Usually, there is a ball after the inauguration and that's it. This year we are holding the (star-studded) show on the night before.

Some firm words of advice to the cast of 'Robin & The 7 Hoods', on Stage 22 of the Warner Bros. lot, several days after the Kennedy assassination:
I have heard some unfortunate remarks on this set about Texas. This indicates that we are still not unified, despite the terrible happenings of the past week. I beg of you not to generalise about people, or make jokes about anyone from Texas. Or say anything that will keep us divided by malice or hatred. Now is the time for all of us to work together with understanding and temperance—and not do or say anything that will prevent that . . .

FRANK SINATRA JOHN F. KENNEDY AND MARIA CALLAS

ME & MY SHADOW

George Evans, eminent publicist, who contributed so much to the Sinatra career in its first decade in the big-time; and to those like Walter O'Keefe (below):

I had to hire a guy to keep my name out of the papers. I was afraid things were getting saturated publicity-wise. Then the factions started. The Bing faction would throw up their arms and say: 'Who does this new guy Sinatra think he is?' And my faction would scream: 'Crosby's finished—our guy'll go further!' There were fist-fights in bars and things. Bing and I had a real war going. We'd say things about each other to stir things up, but through it all, and ever since in fact, we've been the best of friends.

I remember my first club date in New York. Still 1942. At the Rio Bomba. I had to open the show walking round the tables and singing. There was no stage or anything and the dance-floor was only as big as a postage stamp. I was as nervous as hell again, but I sang a few songs and went off. Walter O'Keefe was the star of the show and he was to do his act last. That night he just walked on and said: 'Ladies and gentlemen, I was your star of the evening. But tonight, in this club, we have all just seen a star born'. And he walked out without saying another word. I hadn't really been conscious of any great reception or anything during my act—maybe because I was so nervous—but next day there was a big explosion in all the papers and all round. Dean Martin followed me at that club, I remember, but it closed three days after he started—not his fault as he hadn't had too much experience, he was young, and anyway the club people figured, wrongly, that boy singers were coming in.

. . . and talking of backroom boys, how about a word or two of praise for Bert Allenberg (Bert . . .?) of the William Morris Agency . . .
You never heard of him, but he was a former Australian opera singer who became a vocal coach. If it hadn't been for his coaching when my voice was about gone, I'd have had no career. He did it for nothing because I had nothing to give him at the time.

FRANK SINATRA WITH DEAN MARTIN

I'LL BUY THAT DREAM

Money doesn't interest me.

Money never really interested me, and doesn't now. I made a lot of money working but I never worked hard just to make money. I like to spend money. That's what it's for.

Money—you gotta spend it. Move it around.

There's three things I don't talk about—women, money and photographers . . .!

Sinatra ratings: 1. Recordings. 2. Movies. 3. Night Clubs. 4. TV. How come . . .?
Music is so wonderful to work with. It was really my first love. I guess that's why I place it at the top of the list.

It's very difficult, very tough, for a young singer to come up nowadays and know very much

about the business. Too many of them are breaking in on a fluke record, with echo chambers and all the phoney stuff, and then trying to stay alive without knowing what the hell they're doing. If there were at least six or eight orchestras playing today around the nation, and you had six or eight boy singers, one with each band, then they would have a chance to grow, to serve their apprenticeship . . .
(1965)

Some stimulating etceteras . . .:
Every time a new song comes along, you have a whole new excitement again. That's what makes entertaining an interesting business. No day is the same. Generally, what performers look for most is variance. If not, they should. It keeps you and the audience interested.

I loved pictures like 'Man With The Golden Arm' because I played an interesting character. And I enjoy musicals. I don't think musicals ever will come back in the sense of the way they were. Now I prefer a story with songs. If it were possible, I'd like to do 'Born Yesterday' as a film with songs, with Barbra Streisand. I'm at a good age to play Harry Brock, and it would make it more interesting not to have a good-looking girl, but a girl like Barbra, so people would wonder why he's hung up on her.

EV'RYBODY HAS THE RIGHT TO BE WRONG

Sinatra speaking:
After I fly off the handle and a thing is over, I feel twice as bad as when I was angry.

Enough has happened to me, more than I deserve—all I'd ever want to use the rest of my life. Now I would just like peace of mind.

It happens that I thrive on work. You know why? Because I rest while I work. I don't fight it. I've got a little trick called 'First things first'.

. . . a smoggy day . . .
I've had it with Los Angeles and Hollywood. The smog is so bad I had to visit my doctor three days a week because my nose and throat are affected by it. The air isn't fit to breathe. I haven't got too many years of singing left and I have to take care of myself.

There's no public transportation system. The opera and symphony go begging for money and the museum can't get great paintings to put on the wall. The whole city needs cleaning up.

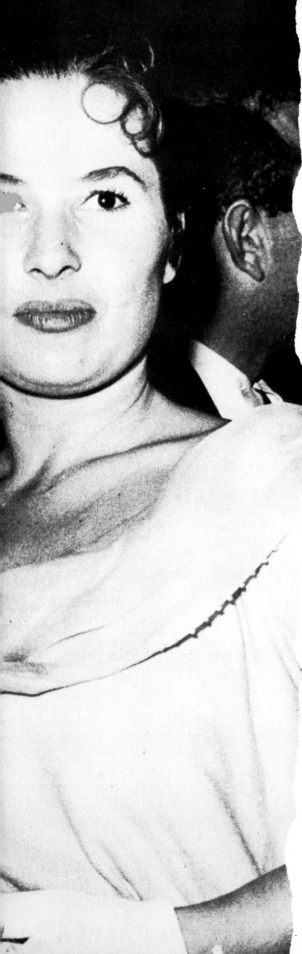

NANCY, THE FIRST

— THE GIRL NEXT DOOR —

Nancy is a noble woman. She's done a magnificent job of raising the kids. And daughter Nancy said: 'In all the years I can remember, Mom has never said an unkind thing about my father'.

Nobody comes before my wife Nancy. That goes for now and for all time . . . (1943)

Nancy and I had a long talk. We've never had anything but kind words. We're always friendly. But there's no reconciliation.

My wife is the most understanding and tolerant woman in the world. Just visualise what I have gone through in recent years and try to imagine how a wife can stand by, faithfully, continue encouragement, and raise a family. Believe me, sometimes I've sweated blood . . .

With Nancy, it was a question of time and pressure. And perhaps those two things make up the unknown quantity which causes a marriage to break up.

I have no regrets. I still think of Nancy whenever I sing or hear 'Nancy With The Laughing Face'. I wrote it for my daughter, really, but it's a sort of family song.

NANCY SINATRA

LOVE & MARRIAGE

(. . . can you have one without the other . . .?
Divorce is not the end of the world, but it hurts.
(1965)

**Onstage, Odeon, Leicester Square, for London
première of 'Me & The Colonel', in aid of
charity . . .:**
I'm here in London solely for this film, the
charity of tonight's showing and to introduce
the cast. I did not come here to get married.

**. . . and an afterthought, at the event which
raised £23,000 for the British Cancer Fund:**
Some of your newspapers would have me
marry as often as King Farouk, and I'm not
even as fat as he is.

Marriage—The Impossible Dream . . .?
I don't say that marriage is impossible, but if I
did marry, it would have to be somebody out of
show business, or somebody who will get out of
the business. I feel I'm a fairly good provider.

All I ask is that my wife looks after me, and I'll
see that she is looked after.

I don't feel that I've ever been a demanding
man, but in some respects I'm a hard man to
live with. I live my life certain ways that I could
never change for a woman. I am a symmetrical
man, almost to a fault. I demand everything in
its place. My clothing must hang just so. There
are some things I can't stand in women. Strong
colognes, for example, drive me out of the
room. First of all I've got an allergy to them. I
begin to sneeze, which is not very
romantic—and this certainly might annoy a
woman. (1965)

Some practical advice on broken engagements:
If the engagement is off, I'll have the ring and
fur coat back, please.

Just Mia and me . . .
We just decided to get married last week. It
seemed right. We were in love and it seemed
logical.

This is a big day fellas. I can't think of what to
say. Let's break out the wine and caviar.

I think I handled it pretty good.

We just decided to get married this week. I had
business on the Coast and Mia was here
anyhow. (1966)

**one . . . two . . . three marriages . . . how about
a fourth . . .?**
I have no thoughts about it. I wouldn't want to
delve into that. (Early-1970s)

**A typical Sinatra reaction to a newspaper
report which quoted Hope Lange—wrongly—
as saying: 'I'm marrying Frank':**
It's bull. I've been married three times and
that's enough. I'm not getting married again.
(pre-Mia)

**. . . but, when all is said and done, what about
all those lovelies with whom you had, shall we
say, close relationships—Kim Novak, Lauren
Bacall, Juliet Prowse, Lana Turner, Jill St John,
Dorothy Provine, et al . . .?**
I loved them all. I really did.

FRANK SINATRA KISSING JILL ST JOHN

SINATRA AND MIA FARROW ON THEIR WEDDING DAY

I GOT IT BAD

Frank, Ava and the roving reporters . . .
Some advice from Sinatra to the ever-present world's pressmen:
Why can't you leave us alone? You can tell Stateside for me what we do is our business. It's a fine thing when we can't go on a vacation without being chased.

You miserable crumbs! You s.o.b.s!

I honestly don't know what we'll do, but I think you can safely say that Miss Gardner and I will be married.

I'm nuts about her and I don't think it's dead. But it certainly is all up in the air.

I guess it's over if that's what Ava says. It's very sad . . . It's tragic. I feel very badly about it.

If it took seventy-five years to get a divorce, there wouldn't be any other woman.
(1951-1953)

. . . and a particularly earnest telegram from FS to the Los Angeles Mirror-News, who printed

a story that Frank kept a picture of Ava pinned to his dressing room mirror . . .:
It's too bad you're such a lying, low, dishonest reporter.

. . . but a more light-hearted chat with the press at Reno, Nevada . . .
I got sore because I got some pretty rough handling from a couple of guys. They were the exception to the rule, though, for the press has done a lot for me.

AVA GARDNER

PEOPLE, PLACES, PATTER

— A FRIEND OF YOURS —

HANK SANICOLA:
Of the five most important people in my life, Hank Sanicola was one. I couldn't have made it without him. Without his encouragement, I very easily might have tossed in the sponge.

To ED SULLIVAN, with grateful thanks:
I am terribly grateful to you, Ed. If I hadn't said what I did, I would have felt like a traitor to those guys overseas. They were the ones who complained to me about conditions over there and you and I both feel that the GIs come first. I didn't mind taking a few raps if it will result in better things for those swell guys.
(for Sullivan's support of Sinatra's contention that the quality of USO shows was inferior) (1945)

To the audience of the Wedgwood Room, Waldorf Astoria—a prestigious New York début appearance—after silencing a drunken heckler:
Ladies and gentlemen, I like to sing. I'm paid to sing. Those who don't like my voice are not compelled to come and surely are under no obligation to stay.

. . . and further comment, later, of that nerve-racking opening night:
If I hadn't been nervous, I'd be a self-satisfied guy and that would stink. (1943)

. . . and again:
Sorry, mister, but there'll be no solo swooning here tonight!

An auspicious concert appearance before President Nixon and the Italian Prime Minister at the White House:
I'm honoured and privileged to be here. Today after the rehearsal I looked at the paintings of President and Mrs Washington and thought about the modest dignity of the Presidency up through the years to now and our President. It makes me very proud of my country. Thank you, Mr President for inviting me here.

TELEVISION
— WHEN NO ONE CARES? —

For me, TV can't work until they fatten up the executive and creative side. How can you put your career in the hands of an idiot who, in the course of an hour, can blow your whole future? The way they get fine artists and throw them around. Take the Judy Garland Show. I adore Judy and think she's one of the greatest living performers—but look what they did to her! A tasteless hack show for an artist like that . . .!

My blood boils when I see the mediocrities who are sitting at the top of the TV networks; refugees from ad. agencies who think that show business is stuck together with spit and gimmicks. These mediocrities at the top hire other mediocrities to work for them so that there isn't any contest to make them look bad. In TV, mediocrities have inherited the earth.

A show like 'Our Town' which I did last year (1954) requires four weeks' rehearsals. And for what? It had a lot of merit, I'll admit, but, after all that work you have nothing to show for it but a bad black-and-white kinescope . . . It's all burned up—poooof!—in ninety minutes. I could make a good movie in that time.

If I fall on my face, I want to be the cause. In my new series, no one has script approval except me. Neither the sponsor nor the network can dictate. They put their money in and that's all.

Man, I've seen TV chew up a lot of talent from a lot of great people. Let's face it, I'm not fond of TV. It takes too much energy, too much tension, havoc and rehearsals for the results you get. I KNOW what it can do to your inside. I had a one-hour weekly show for CBS for a whole year. The only guy I know who has survived and made it pay is Ed Sullivan—the modern Rudy Vallee. Ed is making profit out of 1905 vaudeville. Show him Fink's mules and he'll grab 'em and put 'em out there . . .

FRANK SINATRA WITH JUDY GARLAND

ALL MY TOMORROWS...?

For years I've nursed a secret desire to spend the Fourth of July in a double hammock with a swingin' red-headed broad. But I never could find me a double hammock . . .

One idea I have for the future is to develop more things that don't involve me personally and my talent. I'd like to be able to function more in other departments than I have been able to do in the past. With this new film deal, I want to try and find properties that don't concern me directly. Same thing with my record company—I want to spend more time looking for new talent, soloists, song writers, young guys.

It's kinda hard to stop. You learn to work at a certain pace and if you suddenly slacken off you can get lazy.

I've got all kinds of ideas for the future, but I never like talking about them in case they don't turn out so well. It's been suggested that Elvis and I get together for a TV show or movie. If we found the right script it might be really something.

SHARING THE STAGE WITH ELVIS PRESLEY

Lord knows I've got enough people rushing round working for me that they should be able to come up with something.

. . . and that goes for TV, too . . .:

No longer are we going to heed the slogan of the productive weaklings, 'It can't be done!' That's a lot of poppy-cock. Almost anything can be done in television—or at least tried . . .

Unfortunately not all the top minds in television (and I don't use the word 'top' to mean 'best') are young. We still have some people with the networks, with the talent agencies, with the advertising agencies and among the performers themselves who would rather stick to tried and true formulas. I don't know whether they're just scared or stupid. The competition among shows of our type for guest talent is pretty terrifying. There's a limited quantity to go around, because guests can kill themselves by appearing too often.

Let's face it—the only way to do anything is the right way—and, take my vote for it, the right way to do TV programmes is on FILM!